Research Report
May 2008

I0220681

CONSORTIUM ON CHICAGO SCHOOL RESEARCH AT THE UNIVERSITY OF CHICAGO

From High School to the Future:
ACT Preparation—Too Much, Too Late
Why ACT Scores Are Low in Chicago and What It Means for Schools

Elaine Allensworth, Macarena Correa, and Steve Ponisciak

Acknowledgements

In winter 2005, CCSR researchers asked juniors in three neighborhood high schools to join a longitudinal study of students' making the transition to college. We told students they were the experts who could help us understand how to make Chicago high schools do a better job of supporting students. For three years, students gave up lunch breaks and talked to us about their experiences and plans. Their teachers allowed us to visit their classrooms and gave up free periods to be interviewed. We are indebted to these students and teachers for the many hours of time they volunteered, as well as to the principals and staffs of the high schools in which we worked, who allowed this study to happen and supported it over two years. The students, teachers, and other school staff were the experts who guided our analysis and provided critical insights. In the end, we hope we have delivered on our promise to these students and have assembled their experiences and our analysis into reports that will assist CPS educators and policymakers in improving the high school experience and bridging the gap between students' college aspirations and college success.

We also are indebted to the Chicago Public Schools system for providing us the student record data that allow us to do the quantitative part of this work. In particular, we thank the staff at the Office of Research, Evaluation and Accountability and the Department of Postsecondary Education and Student Development for their efforts in providing data and collaborating with CCSR staff around data issues. A number of individuals and groups at the CPS central office and CPS schools provided feedback on this work as it was in progress. We are very grateful for this feedback, as it helped us frame the findings in a way we hope is useful to practitioners.

This research grew out of the extensive work of the Chicago Postsecondary Transition Project team at the University of Chicago, which is led by Melissa Roderick and included Jenny Nagaoka, Eliza Moeller, Jamiliyah Gilliam, Jonah Deutsch and Vanessa Coca, along with the authors of this report. This team interviewed more than 100 students about their experiences in high school, and our team discussions about those interviews led us to do this investigation into students' ACT score performance. The team continued to provide important feedback as we presented our findings and wrote this report. When interviews were complete, other members of the Postsecondary Transition team transcribed them and did initial coding. We are particularly grateful to Kristin Buller for her work coding interviews, and to Karen Roddie for overseeing much of the transcription.

As always, the CCSR leadership team has provided valuable advice along the way, including feedback on early drafts of the report. This leadership team includes John Q. Easton, Melissa Roderick, Penny Bender Sebring, Sue Sporte, Holly Hart, Stuart Luppescu, Tracy Dell'Angela, and Christopher Mazzeo. We particularly thank CCSR researchers Todd Rosenkranz and Stuart Luppescu for their quick but thorough technical review. Student research assistants Michael Lapido, Alethea Lange and Naphtalia Lafontant helped us gather information on the ACT and other college admissions tests, and we are grateful for their assistance. We would like to thank the Consortium Steering Committee, who participated vigorously in three discussions of this work. Steering committee members Josie Yanguas and Brian Spittle provided helpful comments on a draft of the report. Additionally, James Pellegrino, an educational psychology professor at the University of Illinois at Chicago, reviewed the report at our request, and we are very grateful for his thoughtful, timely feedback.

The public informing staff at CCSR skillfully led this report through all stages of production, and we are indebted to them for their work, particularly Tracy Dell'Angela and Cindy Murphy. We thank Publications & Creative Services at the University of Chicago for editing the report and Jeff Hall for his great work on the layout. We would also like to thank David Shalliol for the fantastic pictures he took of test preparation activities at a CPS high school used throughout this report.

This study was funded by grants from the Bill & Melinda Gates Foundation, the William T. Grant Foundation, and the Spencer Foundation.

Table of Contents

CT STRATEGIES

-bubble inside out
-do what you know
-write in test b
-use process of
-no blank
-be

In the

Brain

NE

SCIENCE

Analyze graphs, table charts, and the answers.
Work from questions to the data.

Underline the clues in the questions.

Let answers tell you where to look.

Math

There are 60 questions.
EASY -to- HARD!
First 30, are the easiest.
If you run out of time always
pick "C".

ENGLISH

SHORTEST IS BEST
10,20,30,40 ARE THE HARDEST
NEVER CHOOSE AN
ANSWER WITH THE
WORD "BEING".
KNOW:
-COMMAS
-SEMICOLONS
-COLONS
-PERIODS
-CONJUNCTION

SLOW READER:
READ FIRST PARAGRAPH, TOPIC SENTENCE, AND
PARAGRAPH.

FAST READER:
READ ENTIRE PASSAGE QUICKLY, SO YOU CAN ANSWER
QUESTIONS SOONER.

Executive Summary

The majority of Chicago Public Schools (CPS) students are not attaining the ACT scores they are aiming for, which they need to qualify for scholarships and college acceptance. In this report we look at the reasons behind students' low performance and what matters for doing well on this test. CPS students are highly motivated to do well on the ACT, and they are spending extraordinary amounts of time preparing for it. Most of the CPS students who took the ACT entered high school with eighth-grade test scores that met state standards and were on par with or better than state and national averages. However, the predominant ways in which students are preparing for the ACT are unlikely to help them do well on the test or to be ready for college-level work. Students are training for the ACT in a last-minute sprint focused on test practice, when the ACT requires years of hard work developing college-level skills.

Key Findings

- **Low ACT scores reflect poor alignment of standards from K–8 to high school and from high school to college.**
  On average, CPS students who take the ACT enter high school meeting state standards and scoring at or above national averages. However, the current standards for high school readiness are not sufficient to be on the path to college. Getting all students college-ready is a goal that has never been met nationally, and performance at the ninth-grade national or state averages is not sufficient. Students have little chance of reaching college-ready benchmarks unless they enter high school exceeding state standards. ACT scores among CPS graduates will continue to fall below college benchmark scores as long as K–8 instruction is aimed at meeting standards that are set too low. Furthermore, not all students are beginning high school meeting state and national expectations, and these students have virtually no chance of making the college readiness benchmarks by the end of the eleventh grade unless they make extraordinary learning gains in high school.

Once in high school, CPS students make smaller improvements on sequential tests from grade to grade than is typical nationally. Students are particularly struggling on the ACT, which is a much more demanding exam than the tests given in earlier grades, the EXPLORE and PLAN. The ACT is more a test of preparation for college than a test of subject matter knowledge. It requires students to have strong problem-solving skills, drawing on a deep understanding of the concepts being tested. The broad content coverage that is typical in high school classes is not sufficient preparation for the ACT or for the demands of college course work. The low scores that students receive on the ACT indicate that students are not sufficiently learning these analytic skills while in high school. Schools vary considerably in the degree to which all students' course work is strongly geared towards preparing students for college. Regardless of the backgrounds of the students they serve, the more that schools develop a college-going culture where teachers work to prepare all students to succeed in college, where students feel that all students are being pushed to prepare for the future, and where students report that their class work is preparing them for college, the higher their students' ACT scores.

- **Test strategies and item practice are not effective mechanisms for improving students' ACT scores.**

Students are highly motivated to prepare for the ACT, but this motivation is being directed at test practice and learning test-taking skills—strategies that are not likely to produce large improvements in test scores. While we find there is some benefit to timed test practice and practice on the English subject test, the effects of practice are modest and diminish once students have initial familiarity with the test. There is no evidence that scores benefit from learning testing strategies or from practicing on test questions outside of taking a full, timed practice test. In fact, improvements from the PLAN to the ACT are smaller the more time teachers spend on test preparation in their classes and the more they use test preparation materials. Furthermore, the ways in which some teachers are using practice tests, particularly the use of the PLAN as a "pre-ACT,"

are likely to give students a false sense of the real exam. Teachers need better strategies for preparing their students for this challenging high-stakes test. Using class time to practice the test is not producing higher scores.

- **ACT performance is directly related to students' performance in their courses.**

The focus on testing strategies and practice diverts students' and teachers' efforts from what really matters—deep analytic work in academic classes. The strongest predictor of improvements from one Educational Planning and Assessment System (EPAS) test to another is the grade students receive in the corresponding subject course. Regardless of whether they start the year with low or high test scores, students who receive higher grades in their English course show higher improvements on the English and reading subject tests; those who receive higher grades in their math course show higher improvements on the math subject test; those who receive higher grades in their science course show higher improvements on the science test. Correspondingly, EPAS improvements are higher the more that school staff are able to get students engaging in appropriate academic behaviors (coming to class, doing their homework, paying attention). Of course, it is not just getting students to work hard that matters, but getting them to do the deep problem-solving work tested on the ACT. Students' improvements from PLAN to ACT are higher the more that their teachers' instructional practices reflect "best practices" in their subject aligned with the ACT. Ironically, the emphasis on test practice takes away from instructional time that could be used for deep analytic class work. Particularly in English, many eleventh-grade teachers feel that ACT preparation interferes with their ability to teach their subject.

- **Incorporating the ACT into high school accountability is not an effective strategy for high school reform by itself, without accompanying strategies to work on instructional practice.**

Concern about high-stakes tests often focuses on the low standards required by large testing programs. The ACT is a very demanding test with real-world consequences for students. It tests the deep problem-solving skills that students need to be successful in college and in the workforce. However, incorporating this test into high stakes accountability for schools has not led to instructional practices that teach more high-level skills. To the contrary, schools and teachers have responded to the ACT in much the same way as seen with tests of low-level skills—emphasizing testing skills, practicing test questions, and doing broad shallow content coverage. The real-world stakes and unusual test structure lead students and teachers to react in ways that accentuate the known problems of high-stakes testing. The EPAS system itself is poorly understood and widely misused, further exacerbating low-level instructional practice.

Introduction

How do we get students to be college-ready? To support CPS as they work to better prepare their students for life after high school, the Consortium on Chicago School Research (CCSR) has been engaged in a multifaceted study of the factors affecting Chicago students' postsecondary outcomes. In 2006, CCSR produced the first of a series of reports on the transition from high school to college: *From High School to the Future: A First Look at Chicago Public School Graduates' College Enrollment, College Preparation, and Graduation from Four-Year Colleges*. In that first report, we showed that the vast majority of CPS students wanted to obtain bachelor's degrees, but only 59 percent of graduates from CPS entered college, only 34 percent entered four-year colleges, and only 35 percent of those who entered four-year colleges graduated with a bachelor's degree within six years. That first report concluded that students' qualifications were the major barrier to college entrance and success, but even CPS students who were qualified for four-year colleges often failed to enroll. In March of this year, CCSR released another report, *From High School to the Future: Potholes on the Road to College*, showing why qualified CPS students do not make it to enrollment at four-year colleges. In this report, we examine one aspect of the low qualifications problem—why so many CPS students are not attaining the ACT scores they need to qualify for scholarships and college acceptance, and what matters for doing well on this test.

As more students than ever before aspire to college, college admissions tests—the ACT and the SAT—have become a significant concern for increasing numbers of students. Admissions tests are one important factor for acceptance to many colleges and universities, and can determine eligibility for many scholarships.[1] Beyond college, businesses offering lucrative positions sometimes reserve a space for test scores on their applications, and college

From High School to the Future: The Chicago Postsecondary Transition Project

In 2004, the Consortium on Chicago School Research began a new longitudinal stream of research, the Chicago Postsecondary Transition Project. The project uses a mixed-methods approach, collecting both quantitative and qualitative data to answer questions about the transition from high school to college. The quantitative data are used to track the experiences of successive cohorts of CPS students from the eleventh grade through college and to systematically analyze the relationships among high school preparation, college choice, and postsecondary outcomes. Data are available from student transcripts, achievement test scores, surveys of students and teachers, and college enrollment records. With these data, we examine how course work shapes student performance in high school and college, how high schools develop skills and qualifications among students, and how access to academic and social supports in high schools shapes college choice and enrollment. The project's qualitative component follows a diverse group of students from three Chicago high schools from eleventh grade until two years after high school graduation. In addition to the postsecondary planning experiences, we are examining differences in the educational demands students face through linked observations of classrooms in both high school and college.

To date we have released two reports from this research initiative:

- ***From High School to the Future: A First Look at Chicago Public School Graduates' College Enrollment, College Preparation, and Graduation from Four-Year Colleges***
In 2006, CCSR released its first major report from the Postsecondary Transition Project, which served as a baseline view of CPS's initiatives to provide college readiness for its graduates. The report looked at why many CPS students were not making the transition to college despite high aspirations. We found that student qualifications as measured by ACT scores and grades constrained students' access to college and undermined their success once enrolled. Graduation rates were low even among students enrolled in four-year colleges. We saw variation in graduation rates among students with similar qualifications depending on their college choice and found that high school grades continued to be strong determinants of graduation. Students with GPAs lower than 3.0 graduated at very low rates regardless of the institution in which they enrolled.

- ***From High School to the Future: Potholes on the Road to College***
In March 2008, CCSR released its second report from the transition project. This report examined CPS students' college search and application process, and barriers they faced translating aspirations to enrollment. We found that low access to social capital (norms, information, and clear structures of support) made managing the process of identifying colleges that matched student qualifications and interests difficult. While students were motivated to enroll in college, they were not taking the steps to complete college applications and secure financial aid. Even though students qualified for admissions, many who hoped to obtain bachelor's degrees did not even apply to four-year institutions. Students who did apply and were accepted often did not enroll. Applying for financial aid was the most significant predictor of whether students who were accepted actually enrolled, particularly for the most highly qualified students.

graduates might place them on their resumes.[2] Meanwhile, a multimillion dollar industry prepares many high school students to take these exams.[3] Clearly college admissions tests hold psychological and economic importance in the United States.[4] In Illinois, the ACT exam holds particular importance, as students' scores are used as the primary indicators of high school performance for state and federal accountability. Thus, students, teachers, and school administrators all have reasons to be concerned about performance on this high-stakes test.

The ACT has been part of the Illinois state assessment for high schools—the Prairie State Achievement Examination (PSAE)—since 2001. Despite substantial concern that students in Chicago's schools score well below expectations, there has been little improvement in average scores over the last five years.[5] In this report, we examine the ways in which CPS high schools are approaching the ACT to understand why scores remain low. Common explanations for poor performance include inadequate academic preparation prior to high school, little rigor in high school course work, low student motivation, and insufficient preparation for the test. We consider these explanations, providing evidence about the degree to which each explains students' low scores. This report shows how students are preparing for the ACT in Chicago and considers the efficacy of the approaches taken by students, teachers, and schools.

This examination of the ways in which teachers and schools are preparing students for the ACT also ends up providing a case study of school reactions to a challenging high-stakes assessment. Researchers and educators have expressed concern about the effects of high-stakes tests on classroom instruction, but much of this concern deals with the focus on low-level skills covered by these assessments. The ACT is not a test of basic skills, but a challenging college-preparatory exam with real-world consequences. It has been suggested that rigorous tests measuring skills needed in the real world might be successful at getting schools to improve their instructional rigor and provide valid assessments of learning.[6] This report shows how students, teachers, and schools have reacted to this challenging test and discusses the implications for teaching practice.

Prairie State Achievement Examination

The PSAE that was taken by students in 2005 had three components: (1) the ACT and its subject tests (English, math, reading, and science),[7] (2) ACT-developed Work Keys tests in reading and math, and (3) Illinois State Board of Education (ISBE)–developed tests in science.[8] It was administered over two days; students took the ACT on the first day and the other portions of the test on the second day.

ISBE organizes students' performance by their scores on both days of the test into four categories: Exceeds, Meets, Below, and Warning. For each subject, students' ACT subject test scores and a corresponding Work Keys or ISBE test score is converted to a raw score based on the number of questions answered correctly. Scores are standardized, then averaged over the two days of the test. For example, the reading PSAE score comes from the ACT reading test and the reading Work Keys test weighted equally.[9] The standardization allows for PSAE scores to be comparable over time.[10]

For more information, see the Illinois State Board of Education: www.isbe.net/assessment/psae.htm, and the Consortium on Chicago School Research: *Understanding the Prairie State Achievement Exam: A Descriptive Report with Analysis of Student Performance:* ccsr.uchicago.edu/content/publications.php?pub_id=9.

The 2007–08 PSAE administration schedule is as follows:[11]

DAY 1 Wednesday, April 23, 2008
ACT English—45 minutes (75 questions)
ACT Mathematics—60 minutes (60 questions)
[required 15-minute break]

ACT Reading—35 minutes (40 questions)
ACT Science—35 minutes (40 questions)
[required 15-minute break]

ACT Writing—30 minutes (1 prompt)

DAY 2 Thursday, April 24, 2008
ISBE-Developed Science—40 minutes (45 questions)
Work Keys Applied Mathematics—45 minutes (33 questions)
[required 15-minute break]

Work Keys *Reading for Information*—45 minutes (33 questions)

CPS Students' ACT Scores Do Not Meet Their College Expectations

The vast majority of CPS students aspire to attain a bachelor's degree; in fact, 78 percent of CPS seniors said that this was their goal in a 2005 survey.[12] However, the average composite ACT score for juniors in 2005 was 17, which is well below the score required by many colleges and most scholarships.[13] The CPS average is also substantially below the national average ACT score of 21.1. Comparison to the national average could be considered unfair because all CPS students take the ACT, while the national statistic is mostly comprised of students who plan to attend college. A fairer comparison is the Illinois average, because all students in Illinois take the ACT. However, the average CPS score is still well below the Illinois average of 20.5.[14]

Not only are students with very low scores unlikely to gain admittance to four-year colleges and access to scholarships, but low scores also indicate that students are unlikely to succeed in college course work. ACT, Inc., has compared students' performance on subject tests of the ACT to their grades in introductory college classes. For each ACT subject test, ACT has set a college readiness benchmark score, at which level a student has a 50 percent likelihood of getting a B or better in an introductory class and a 75 percent likelihood of getting a C or better.[15] Table 1 shows the percentage of CPS juniors who meet these benchmarks, compared to students nationally. In CPS, only 16 percent of students meet the math benchmark of 22 points, compared to 42 percent nationally. This suggests that the vast majority of CPS graduates are not prepared for college algebra. In fact, most CPS students' scores are well below the benchmark in math. As shown in Figure 1, most students score between a 14 and a 17 on the math portion of the ACT; the most common score is a 15.

FIGURE 1

ACT math scores for CPS juniors in 2005

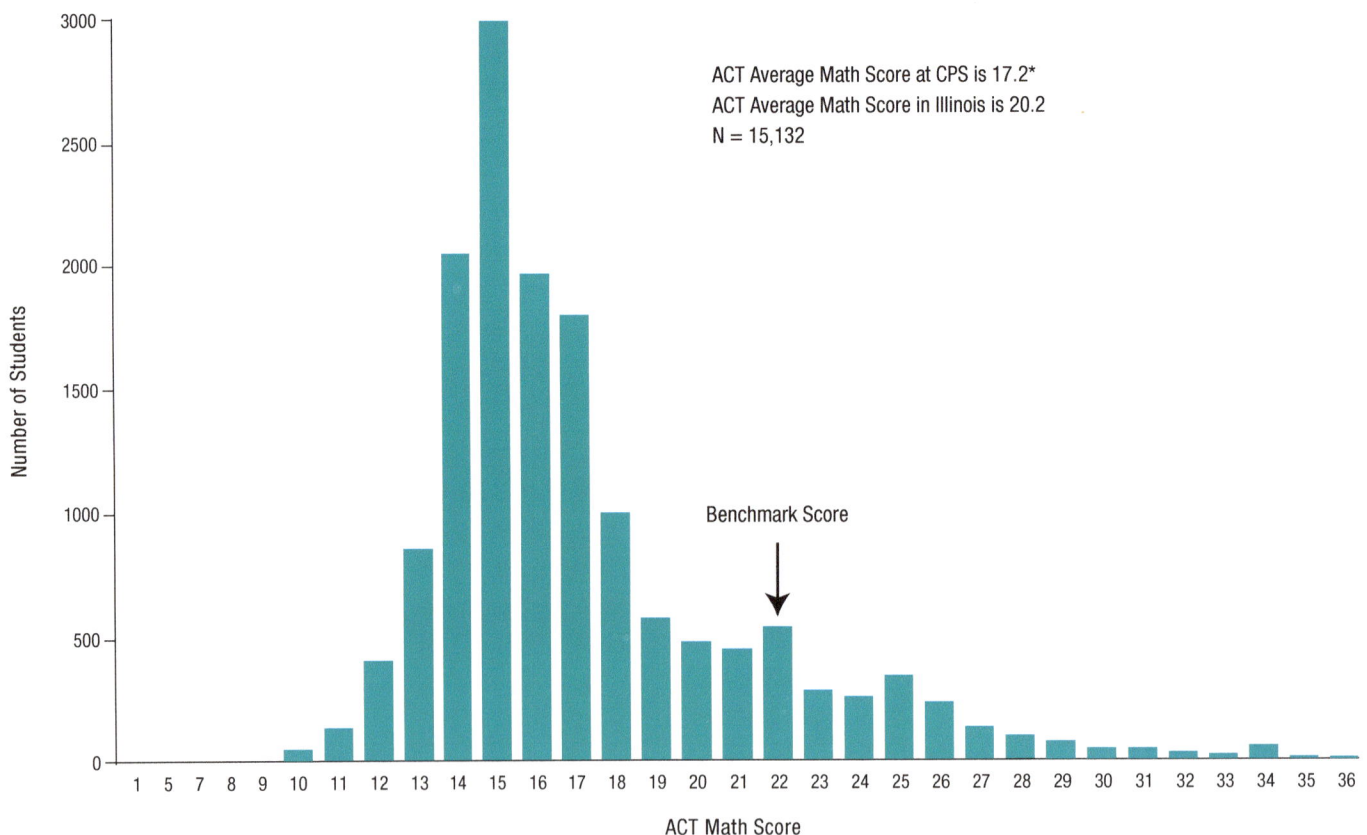

ACT Average Math Score at CPS is 17.2*
ACT Average Math Score in Illinois is 20.2
N = 15,132

*Note: Average score varies slightly from official CPS records because this sample only includes students with fall PLAN scores and grades in subject tested.

TABLE 1

Percentage of CPS students who met ACT college benchmark scores

	CPS	National
Math		
College algebra benchmark = 22	16%	42%
English		
English composition benchmark = 18	43%	69%
Reading		
Introductory social science course benchmark = 21	26%	53%
Science		
College biology benchmark = 24	9%	27%

Note: Benchmark scores correspond to a 50 percent chance of getting a B or better in the corresponding freshman-level college course. The CPS statistics are based on juniors in 2005. The national statistics come from the ACT website (www.act.org/news/releases/2006/ndr.html).

The English benchmark is the lowest of the subject tests at 18, yet fewer than half of CPS juniors (43 percent) score an 18 or higher on the English test, compared to 69 percent of ACT-takers nationally (see Table 1). Figure 2 shows that it is most common for CPS students to score a 14 or 15 on the English test. Only about a quarter of CPS juniors (26 percent) make the reading benchmark of 21 points, compared to about half of students nationally (see Table 1). As shown in Figure 3, most CPS students score well below the reading benchmark, suggesting that they will struggle in college social studies courses. Only the very top CPS students (9 percent) meet the science benchmark, which is the highest benchmark at 24 points (see Figure 4). The average CPS student scores 18 points on the science subject test.

FIGURE 2

ACT English scores for CPS juniors in 2005

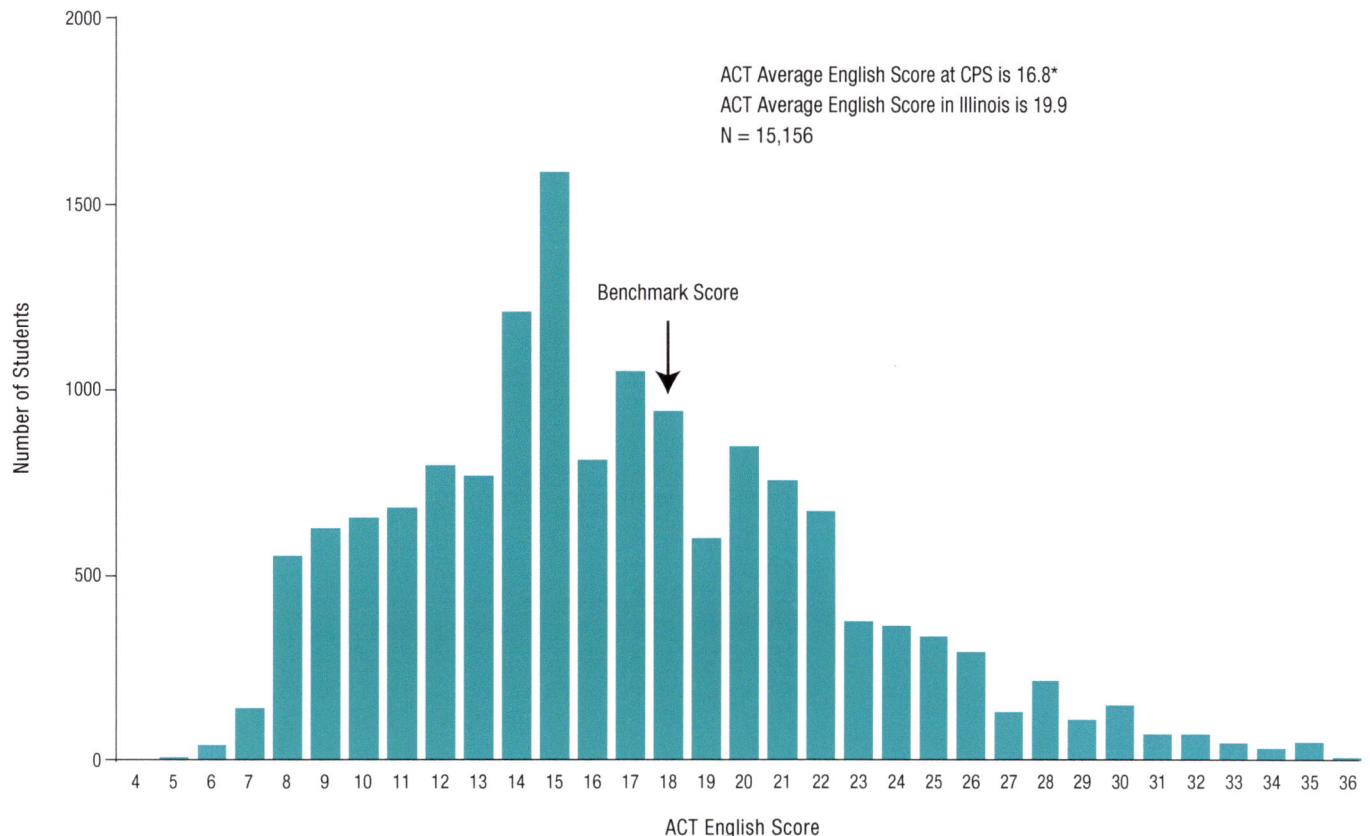

ACT Average English Score at CPS is 16.8*
ACT Average English Score in Illinois is 19.9
N = 15,156

Benchmark Score

*Note: Average score varies slightly from official CPS records because this sample only includes students with fall PLAN scores and grades in subject tested.

FIGURE 3

ACT reading scores for CPS juniors in 2005

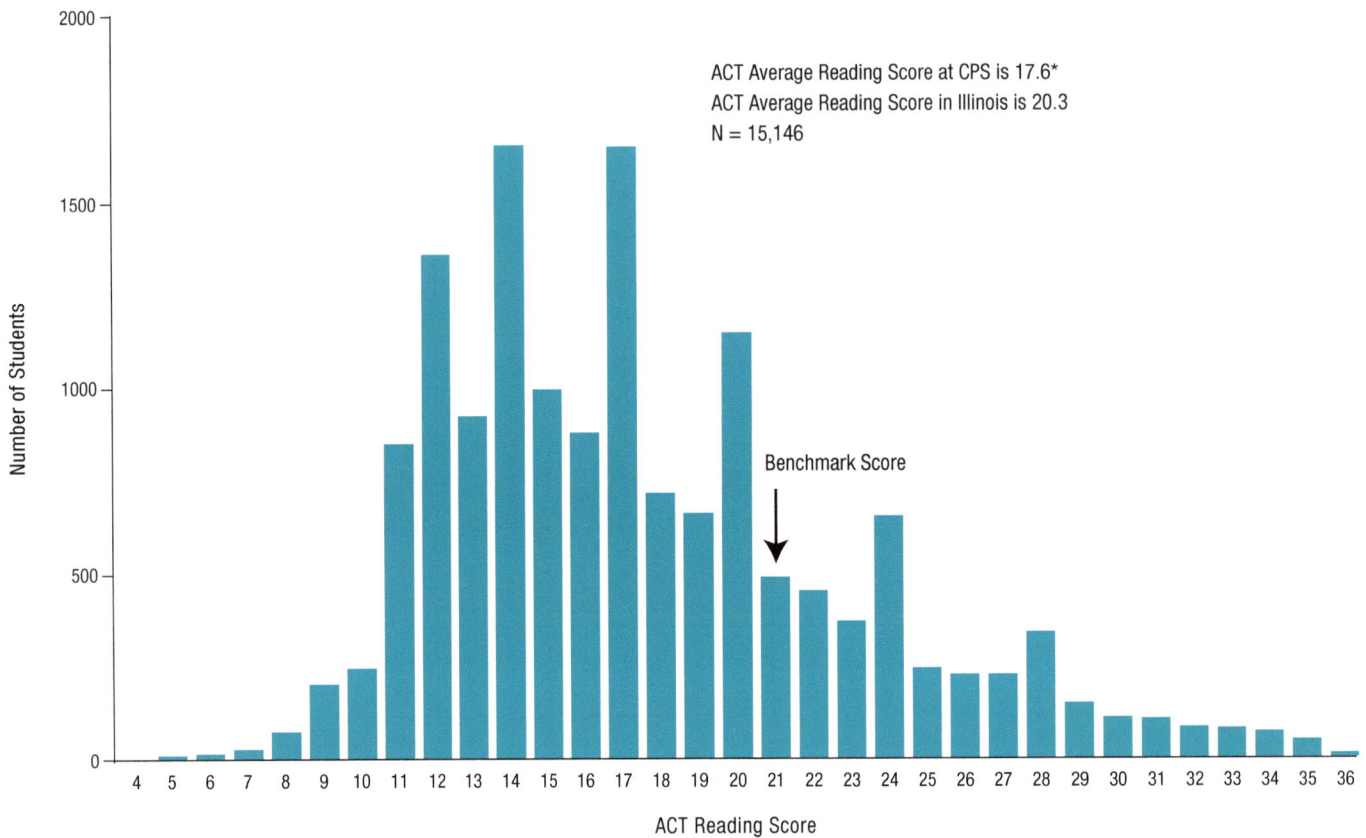

ACT Average Reading Score at CPS is 17.6*
ACT Average Reading Score in Illinois is 20.3
N = 15,146

Benchmark Score

Number of Students

ACT Reading Score

*Note:** Average score varies slightly from official CPS records because this sample only includes students with fall PLAN scores and grades in subject tested.

CPS students' scores are not only below their aspirations for college, but also below their expectations. In our 2007 survey, we asked students what ACT score they would be satisfied with—more than 80 percent said they would be satisfied with a score of 20 or higher. Yet in the past two years, only 20 percent received a score this high. At the same time, only 5 percent of students said they would be satisfied with an ACT composite score of 17, yet this was the CPS average. From our interviews in 2005, we saw that students rarely met their goal ACT score; 80 percent of our interview sample performed lower on the ACT than they expected, and almost 80 percent of the interviewed students expressed an interest in retaking the ACT with hopes of getting a better score. After receiving their scores, students began to change their college plans. The stories were discouraging:

In March (before the ACT)

Interviewer: Do you know what score you're shooting for?
Student: At least the mid 20's.
Interviewer: Any reason?
Student: So I can pick my own colleges…. If I don't want to go to Daley [a community college], I don't have to go to Daley. I can go to, like I said, [University of Illinois] Champaign or even a better place.

In May (after the ACT)

Interviewer: Do you have a list of schools that you're going to apply to, that you're interested in?
Student: Well, right now I'm basically going to go to Daley for like, the first year and a half, so I can get the general, basic classes, and then transfer them out to . . . IIT, I guess.
Interviewer: Do you think it's going to be hard to get into IIT?
Student: I have a 3.5, and I have a 25 percent [class rank]. The only problem will be the ACT, 'cause I got a 16 on it. [The student needs a 21 to get into the IIT program.]

FIGURE 4

ACT science scores for CPS juniors in 2005

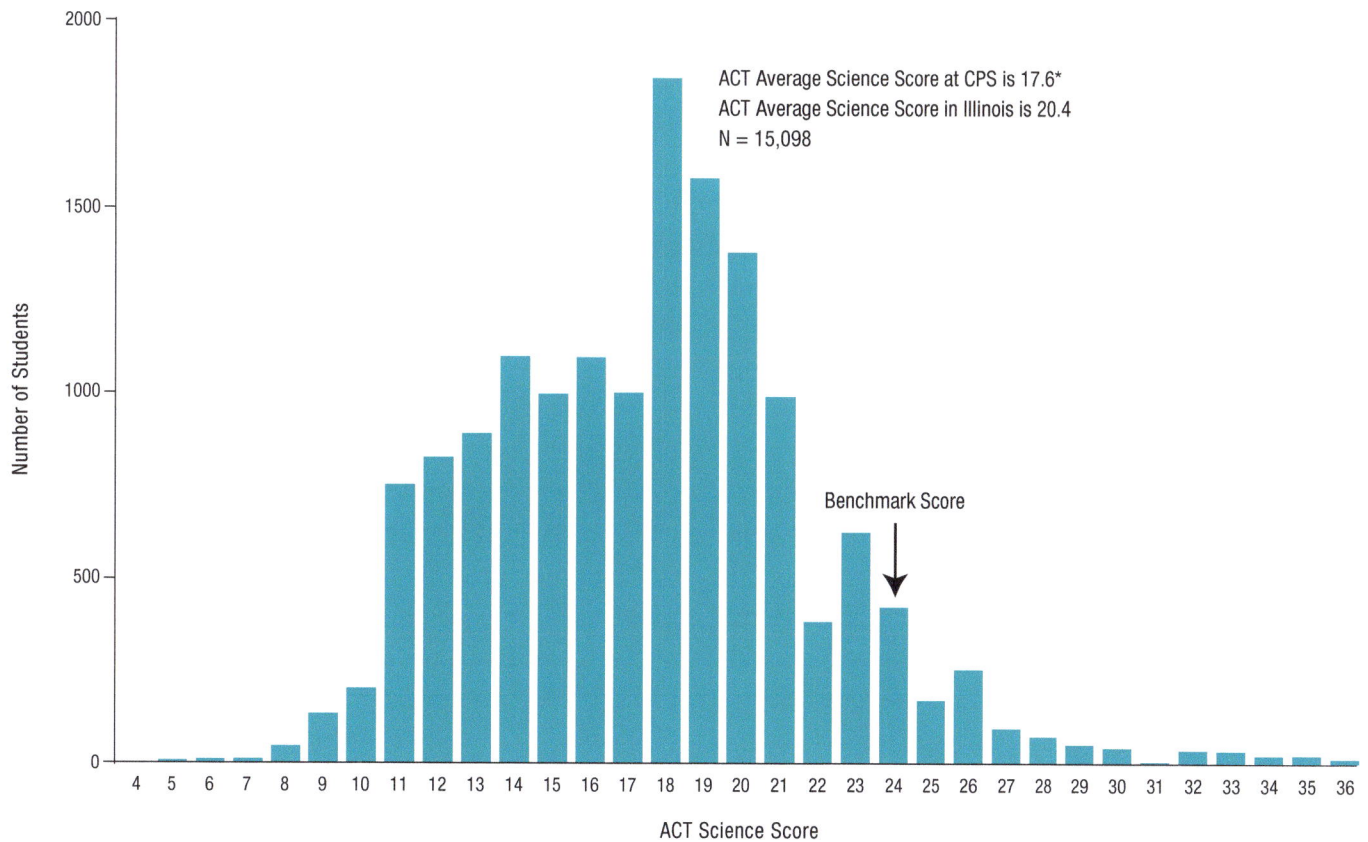

ACT Average Science Score at CPS is 17.6*
ACT Average Science Score in Illinois is 20.4
N = 15,098

Benchmark Score

Number of Students

ACT Science Score

*Note: Average score varies slightly from official CPS records because this sample only includes students with fall PLAN scores and grades in subject tested.

Data Used in This Report

This report draws on two main sources of data: (1) a quantitative data set following CPS students who were in eleventh grade in spring 2005, and (2) a qualitative longitudinal sample of 105 of those students who were in eleventh grade in spring 2005. The students were interviewed at multiple points, including the winter of eleventh grade (about a month before taking the ACT), the end of the eleventh grade, and the fall of twelfth grade. Additional quantitative data come from students who were in eleventh grade in 2007. Teacher survey data from 2005 and 2007 also were used.

Quantitative Data

A wide range of quantitative data was incorporated into this analysis, including CPS administrative, transcript, and test data; CCSR surveys; ACT data; and National Student Clearinghouse (NSC) data. We used achievement test scores from multiple school years, starting with tests students took in the eighth grade in spring 2002—the Iowa Tests of Basic Skills (ITBS) and the Illinois Standards Achievement Test (ISAT). In the fall of ninth grade, students took the EXPLORE, and in both the fall of tenth grade and the fall of eleventh grade they took the PLAN. (See Chapter 3.) Student grades are an important component of many analyses. In cases where grades predict ACT composite scores, weighted GPAs from student transcripts were used. When subject-specific ACT scores are discussed, unweighted grades from corresponding courses were used in the analyses. NSC data helped inform the relationship between ACT benchmarks and college retention for CPS students.

CCSR conducts citywide biannual surveys. The 2005 administration included a survey specific to juniors containing questions about the PSAE. Eleventh-grade students in 77 high schools and teachers of eleventh-graders in 72 high schools completed this survey in the spring of 2005 (11,003 students and 4,142 teachers). As a supplement to this survey, we incorporated more recent information on ACT preparation and scores from the eleventh-graders and their teachers from surveys given in spring 2007. The 2007 survey asked more detailed questions on the ACT than did the survey in 2005. Eleventh-grade students in 96 schools and teachers of eleventh-graders in 74 high schools completed the 2007 survey (13,920 students and 4,660 teachers). In both survey years, students were asked about the emphasis of the PSAE/ACT in their schools, and teachers were asked about test preparation in their classes. Additional survey data were included from high school students in all grades to measure other aspects of school climate.

Qualitative Sample

In winter 2005, researchers at the Consortium on Chicago School Research began a multiyear study of the transition from high school to college (see "From High School to the Future: The Chicago Postsecondary Transition Project," page 6). Qualitative data presented in this report are drawn from a sample of 105 students. We recruited students as juniors from three CPS high schools. The students in our longitudinal qualitative sample roughly reflect the demographic diversity of CPS students. The sample is gender-balanced (51 percent male, 49 percent female) and includes students from each major racial/ethnic group in CPS (49 percent African American, 47 percent Latino, 2 percent white, 2 percent Asian). Students in the sample live in different neighborhoods throughout Chicago, entered high school with a range of incoming achievement test scores, and accumulated very different qualifications for college in terms of their grades and ACT scores. Students also participated in a variety of curricular tracks throughout high school. To thoroughly understand the outcomes of high-achieving high school graduates, we oversampled students in the International Baccalaureate (IB) program, as well as students taking honors and Advanced Placement (AP) courses.

This report uses interviews conducted twice during the spring of junior year, once before and once after taking the ACT. Initial interviews occurred within the month immediately preceding the state accountability test, the Prairie State Achievement Examination (PSAE). Students responded to questions about what they were doing to prepare for the upcoming exam, how well they thought they would do on the exam, and the types of scores they needed to meet their goals for college. The second round of interviews occurred in May 2005, after students had received their ACT scores. Information about retaking the ACT comes from a third set of interviews conducted in students' twelfth-grade year.

We also interviewed 24 teachers in our field schools who taught core classes (English, math, and social science) attended by students in our interview sample. Frequently, students and teachers in our data were discussing the same class. Teachers were asked about PSAE preparation in their classrooms, in addition to general questions about their perspectives on postsecondary education for their students and curriculum.

Chapter 1

Why Are ACT Scores So Low?

Why do CPS students perform so poorly on the ACT? To answer this question, we examined a number of potential explanations. Maybe students started off far behind in elementary school and never caught up to expected standards. Thus, they were unprepared for high-school-level work. Or maybe they were ready for high school, but the work they did in their high school courses did not prepare them well for college, as reflected by low scores on the ACT. Alternatively, maybe their scores underestimated their actual preparation for college—they were underperforming on the test relative to their true academic skills. Maybe students lacked motivation to try hard and prepare for the test, or they spent too little time preparing for the test. Finally, it could be that the ways in which students prepared for the test were ineffective for improving their scores. This chapter explores all but one of these potential explanations, showing the degree to which each is supported by evidence. The final issue—how students prepare for the test—is discussed in Chapter 2.

Are ACT Scores Low Due to Poor Academic Preparation for High School?

There are three tests that we can use to gauge whether students who took the ACT in 2005 were ready for high-school-level work when they entered the ninth grade. At the end of eighth grade, CPS currently uses the state accountability test—ISAT—to measure students' skills in reading and math. When the class of 2006 was in eighth grade, there was an additional test given at the end of each school year used for district accountability, the ITBS. We can see to what extent juniors who took the ACT in 2005 were performing below expectations on those tests when they were in eighth grade, before they entered high school. CPS also administers an ACT-designed test, the EXPLORE, to all ninth-grade students at the start of the ninth-grade year. Because it is administered at the beginning of the school year, this exam can also help us gauge students' skills as they began high school.

Test Scores at the End of Eighth Grade among ACT-Takers

Figure 5a shows the distribution of ITBS and ISAT scores among students who took the ACT in spring 2005. Because not all eighth-grade students stay in school until the end of their eleventh-grade year, these averages are higher than the districtwide average eighth-grade test scores. In fact, the majority of the CPS students who took the ACT in spring 2005 scored at or above national norms on the ITBS in reading at the end of their eighth-grade year (55 percent). In addition, two-thirds met the ISAT eighth-grade reading standards when they were in eighth grade (58 percent met standards, 6 percent exceeded them). Thus, most students who took the ACT reading exam in spring 2005 were performing at reading levels that indicated they were prepared for high school, according to two different eighth-grade tests.

However, the vast majority of the CPS students who met the expected criteria on the eighth-grade reading tests did not meet the reading benchmark on the ACT in the eleventh grade (Figure 5b). Of the 58 percent of students *who met the ISAT standards* in reading (but did not exceed them), only about a quarter (24 percent) met the ACT reading benchmark three years later. About 88 percent of the students who exceeded ISAT reading standards in eighth grade met the ACT benchmark in reading; however, only 6 percent of ACT-takers exceeded ISAT standards in eighth grade. Of the 55 percent of students who performed at or above national norms on the ITBS reading exam in eighth grade, only one-third (34 percent) met the ACT reading benchmark at the end of eleventh grade. These students were in the top half of the national distribution in reading performance when they were in eighth grade, yet only 34 percent of them met the ACT benchmark three years later.

A similar picture can be seen in students' math scores. Sixty-one percent of the students who took the ACT in spring 2005 scored at or above national norms on the ITBS math exam in eighth grade. Yet, of these students who scored at the national average or better as eighth-graders, only about one-fifth (21 percent) met the ACT benchmark in math in eleventh grade. These same students were less likely to meet the ISAT standards because the standards were harder in math than in reading in 2002; only 39 percent performed at or above standards on the eighth-grade math ISAT.[16] However, among that subset of students who met standards in ISAT math but did not exceed them, only about one-fifth (21 percent) met the math ACT benchmark three years later. The vast majority of students who exceeded the ISAT standards in eighth grade met the ACT benchmark (85 percent), but only 7 percent of the students exceeded the ISAT math standards when they were in eighth grade.

Thus, while there were some students who were unprepared to do high school work when they entered high school, the majority of juniors who took the ACT in spring 2005 had eighth-grade reading scores that suggested they were ready for high school English according to the state standards and national averages. Most had math scores on the ITBS that were higher than national norms, and almost 40 percent met the state standards in math on the ISAT. Yet, among students whose eighth-grade test scores suggested they were ready for high-school-level work, the majority did not meet the ACT benchmarks in eleventh grade. This suggests either that the eighth-grade benchmarks were set too low to be aligned with the eleventh-grade test or that the preparation students received in high school was not sufficient.[17] It is also possible that the skills tested in eighth grade were much more basic than required to predict performance on the ACT. Therefore, to further examine students' academic preparation as they began high school, we now turn to a test that is aligned with the ACT which CPS students take in the fall of their ninth-grade year.

FIGURE 5A

Eighth-grade test performance of CPS students who took the ACT in eleventh grade

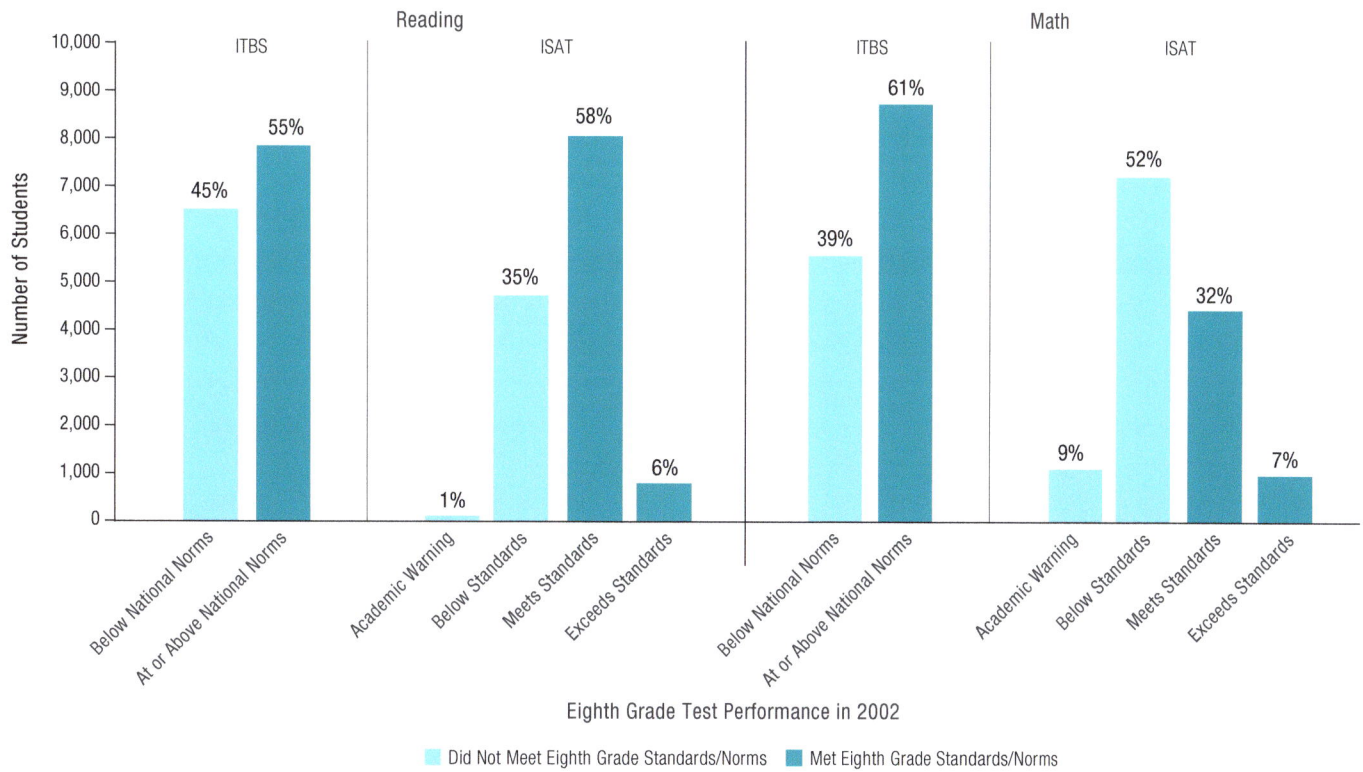

Reading | Math

ITBS | ISAT | ITBS | ISAT

Eighth Grade Test Performance in 2002

■ Did Not Meet Eighth Grade Standards/Norms ■ Met Eighth Grade Standards/Norms

Note: These figures only include students who took both the eighth-grade test and the ACT.

FIGURE 5B

Percentage of students meeting ACT benchmarks in 2005 by their performance on eighth-grade tests

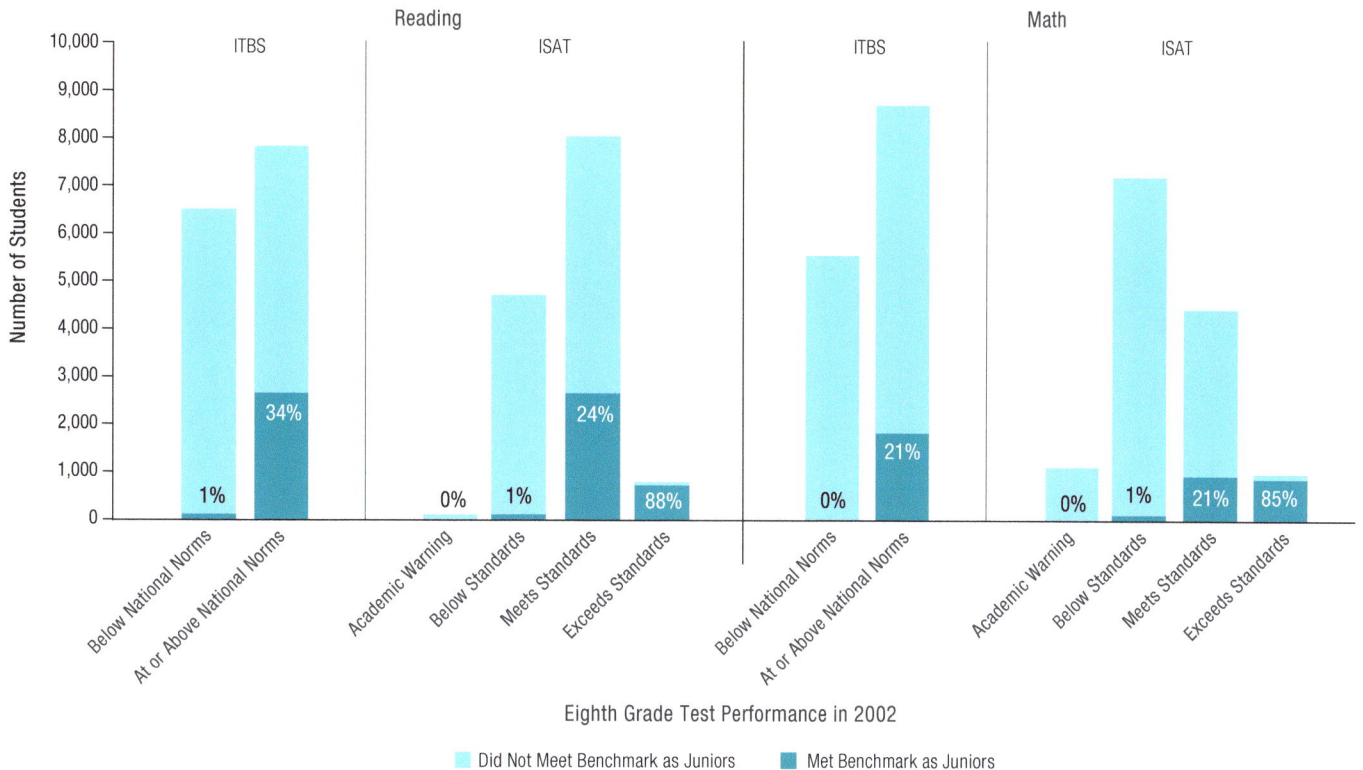

Reading | Math

ITBS | ISAT | ITBS | ISAT

Eighth Grade Test Performance in 2002

■ Did Not Meet Benchmark as Juniors ■ Met Benchmark as Juniors

Note: These figures only include students who took both the eighth-grade test and the ACT.

EPAS Scores at the Start of Ninth Grade among ACT-Takers

CPS uses an ACT-designed sequence of tests, the EPAS, to gauge student performance in grades 9, 10, and 11 (see Table 2). In the fall of ninth grade, students take the EXPLORE, and they take the PLAN in the fall of both tenth and eleventh grades. They then take the ACT in the spring of eleventh grade. We can examine student progress from ninth grade onwards using this series of aligned exams. ACT has identified levels of performance on the EXPLORE and PLAN that correspond to the college benchmark levels on the ACT.[18] Students who are at the benchmark on the EXPLORE have a 50 percent chance of meeting the benchmark score on the ACT.

Table 3 shows the percentage of students who met the EXPLORE and PLAN benchmarks among students who took the ACT in spring 2005. As observed in the eighth-grade tests, CPS students who stayed in school until eleventh grade and took the ACT were not underperforming when they entered high school, compared to the nation as a whole. In CPS, 35 percent of students met the EXPLORE math benchmark, compared to 34 percent of students nationally; 60 percent met the English benchmark, compared to 63 percent nationally; 42 percent met the reading benchmarks, compared to 41 percent nationally; and 10 percent met the science benchmark, compared to 12 percent nationally.

While the academic skills of CPS students who took the ACT were similar to students nationally when they entered high school and were also similar to state averages,[19] these skill levels were not sufficient to meet most of the ninth-grade benchmark scores. Only 35 percent of CPS students who took the ACT in 2005 met the math benchmark on the EXPLORE at the beginning of their ninth-grade year. This suggests that two-thirds were behind where they should have been to have a 50-50 chance of meeting the ACT benchmark score by

TABLE 2

The EPAS schedule in CPS

October of 9th Grade	EXPLORE
October of 10th Grade	PLAN
October of 11th Grade	PLAN
April of 11th Grade	ACT

TABLE 3

Percentage of students meeting benchmark scores on EPAS

Percentage of Students Meeting Benchmarks	Math	English	Reading	Science
9th Grade EXPLORE Benchmark	35%	60%	42%	10%
National Comparison	34%	63%	41%	12%
10th Grade PLAN Benchmark	16%	58%	44%	10%
National Comparison	36%	73%	50%	24%
11th Grade ACT Benchmark	16%	43%	26%	9%
National Comparison	42%	69%	53%	27%

Percentage of Students Making Expected Improvements on Sequential Tests (Based on National Averages)				
9th-10th Grade PLAN Gains	39%	48%	55%	36%
10th-11th Grade PLAN–ACT Gains	36%	36%	28%	35%

Note: CPS statistics based on all 11th graders in Spring 2005 who took all three tests. National statistics on the percentage of students meeting benchmark scores come from ACT documents and do not necessarily include students who took all three tests. National statistics on the percentage of students meeting ACT benchmarks come from an ACT news release (August 16, 2006) on ACT scores for the class of 2006 (corresponding to the graduation year of the CPS cohort being studied). EXPLORE and PLAN national statistics for all but the reading subject test come from a news release from August 18, 2004, corresponding to the year the CPS students were sophomores (ACT, 2004). The national statistics for the reading test were calculated from the norming tables in the technical manuals for the EXPLORE and ACT, and are based on students who took the tests in 2006—several years after the CPS students (ACT, 2007b; ACT, 2007c). ACT does have statistics available for only those students who took all three tests (ACT, 2007e, page 13). However, they only include students who graduated in these statistics, which inflates the rates at which students meet benchmarks. Expected improvements come from the PLAN technical manual (ACT, 2007b), and the EXPLORE technical manual (ACT, 2007c).

the end of eleventh grade. Science performance looks even worse—only 10 percent of CPS students met the science benchmark in ninth grade. This is partly because the science benchmark score is set quite high. Nevertheless, EXPLORE benchmarks are set to indicate probable success on later EPAS tests, suggesting that the vast majority of CPS students would struggle to meet the science benchmark in later years. Only 42 percent of students who took the ACT in 2005 met the reading benchmark on the EXPLORE in ninth grade. This is considerably below the 64 percent that met expectations on the ISAT (see Figure 5), and suggests that the ISAT standard was not well aligned with ACT standards.[20]

Most CPS students who make it to the end of the eleventh grade do not begin high school with the academic skills that ACT, Inc., says they should have to be ready for the ACT. However, this is just the first problem. Even among those CPS students who did meet the ninth-grade benchmark scores, only some managed to reach the benchmark scores on the eleventh-grade ACT. Almost a third of CPS ACT-takers met the math benchmark score at the beginning of ninth grade, but only 16 percent met the benchmark on the ACT. Sixty percent met the English benchmark at the beginning of ninth grade, but only 43 percent met the benchmark at the end of eleventh grade on the ACT. More than 40 percent met the reading benchmark on the EXPLORE, but only 26 percent met the reading benchmark on the ACT. While ninth-grade performance among CPS ACT-takers looks similar to national levels, eleventh-grade performance looks dramatically different in all four subject areas. In all areas but English, the national rates at which students met the benchmark scores on the eleventh-grade ACT were more than double CPS rates; in English they were more than 20 percentage points higher.

The performance gaps between CPS and national rates get larger as high school progresses. However, these are unfair comparisons because the national sample is not consistent over time and the national ACT sample may be overrepresented by students who plan to go to college. There is an alternative way to examine progress on the EPAS system that uses a consistent national sample. Rather than looking at the

percentages of students who met benchmark scores, we can look at the percentage of students who made expected improvements from one test to the next. ACT produces tables of average ACT and PLAN scores based on students who took pairs of tests, EXPLORE and PLAN or PLAN and ACT. [21] By definition, these tables must include students who took both tests. To be consistent with national averages, about half of CPS students should have ACT scores that are at or above the median ACT score of students with the same PLAN score in the national sample. For example, if half of the students in the national sample who scored a 16 on the PLAN received an 18 or higher on the ACT, we would expect half of CPS students who scored a 16 on the PLAN to also score an 18 on the ACT. Likewise, about half of CPS students should have PLAN scores that are at or above the median PLAN score of students with the same EXPLORE score in the national sample.

In two subjects, English and reading, CPS students show improvements that are consistent with those of the national sample from the EXPLORE in ninth grade to the PLAN in tenth grade (see Table 3). However, in math and science, fewer than 40 percent of CPS students make the median national PLAN score for students with matched EXPLORE scores. Furthermore, improvements from the PLAN in the fall of tenth grade to the ACT in the spring of eleventh grade are well below median levels in all subjects. Only about one-third or less of CPS students made the median ACT score in each of the four subject area tests, compared to students nationally with the same PLAN scores. Many students who meet the EPAS benchmarks in the ninth or tenth grade fail to meet ACT benchmarks by the end of eleventh grade.

To summarize, CPS students who take the ACT in eleventh grade have similar academic skills when they enter high school as those students beginning high school nationwide and statewide. However, this level of performance is not sufficient—nationally, most students do not meet ninth-grade benchmark scores in math, reading, or science. Standards used in eighth and ninth grade are set far too low to predict college readiness by the end of eleventh grade. Only students who exceed state standards in the eighth grade have a good chance of meeting ACT benchmark scores, yet few CPS students begin high school exceeding standards. Added to this, CPS students make smaller improvements in test scores over their first three years of high school than do students nationally who began high school with the same skill levels on the ninth-grade EXPLORE exam. Therefore, even many CPS students who seemed ready for high school work at the beginning of ninth grade fail to make the ACT benchmark scores at the end of eleventh grade.

Are ACT Scores Low Due to Inadequate Academic Preparation for College during High School?

The ACT is designed to measure students' readiness for college. Thus, we need to be concerned that low performance on the ACT indicates that the vast majority of CPS graduates do not have the skills they will need in college. Yet, we often hear concern that students' true skills are not measured well by the test.[22] Could it be that CPS students are receiving ACT scores lower than their actual college readiness level? We can try to gauge students' readiness for college in two ways: by comparing students' ACT scores to their grades and by comparing college retention rates for students meeting ACT benchmarks in CPS to students nationally.

ACT Scores by Students' Course Grades

Earlier work at CCSR, as well as studies by ACT and others, have found that high school grades are very strong predictors of college enrollment and college graduation—more important than students' test scores or the extent to which they take advanced course work.[23] Given that grades are such strong predictors of college graduation, we can look at the extent to which students' ACT scores correspond with their course grades. If students' ACT scores are lower than we would expect given their grade point averages, this might suggest that their ACT scores under-predict how they will do in college.

To do this, we compared grades and ACT scores of CPS students to those of a national sample, published by ACT.[24] When we compared students with similar grades and similar racial/ethnic backgrounds, we found that CPS students had ACT scores that were similar

to those of the national sample (see Figure 6). Among students graduating in 2006 with GPAs of 3.5 or better, African American and white CPS students had the same scores as the national sample, on average, while Asian and Latino CPS students had ACT scores only one point lower than their counterparts nationally. At the other end of GPA performance, among students with GPAs of 1.99 or lower, Asian and Latino students had about the same ACT scores as their national counterparts, but African American and white students in CPS had ACT scores one point lower.

While CPS students had similar ACT scores to those of students nationally with similar GPAs and racial/ethnic backgrounds, there were large discrepancies between the national ACT sample and CPS students in the proportion of students with high grades compared to low grades. Among ACT-takers nationally, 41 percent had a GPA of 3.5 or higher—A averages—but within CPS, only 18 percent had GPAs that were this high. Nationally, only 3 percent of ACT-takers had GPAs below a C average (2.0). In CPS, one quarter of ACT-takers had GPAs below 2.0. Granted, the ACT sample is likely more privileged than the average CPS student. However, aspirations to attend college are not substantially different, making the disparity in GPAs among CPS students disheartening. Given that half of CPS graduates have GPAs below 2.5, low ACT scores are not surprising—they are consistent with students' performance in their courses. We show later in this report that improvements on the EPAS system are strongly associated with students' course grades.

Looking at Figure 6 in a slightly different way, we see that there were large differences in ACT scores by race/ethnicity among students with the same high school grades. Among students with a GPA of 3.5 or higher, African American students scored, on average, five points below white students, and Latino students scored three to four points below white students. At lower grade point levels, differences by race/ethnicity also are evident, although they are smaller. This is a disturbing pattern and may suggest possible racial bias in scores. We look into this issue in "A Closer Look at ACT Scores by Race and Ethnicity," on page 25, to understand the reasons behind the differences in ACT performance by race and ethnicity in CPS and in the national samples.

ACT scores by GPA and race/ethnicity: National statistics and CPS

ACT Composite Scores for Students with 3.5 or Higher GPAs
18 Percent of Students in CPS
41 Percent of Students Nationally

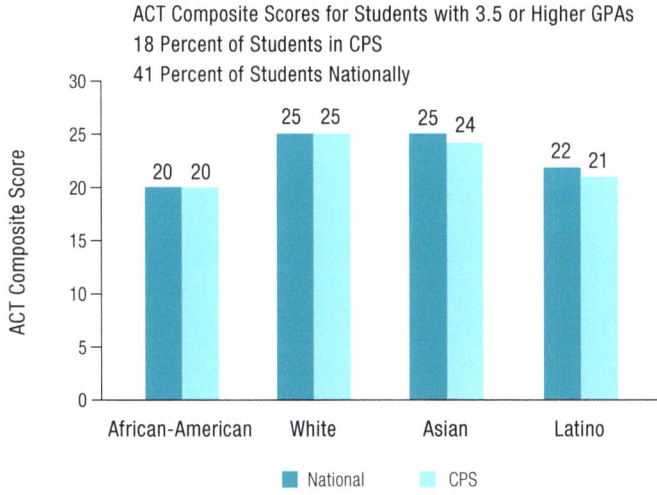

ACT scores by GPA and race/ethnicity: National statistics and CPS

ACT Composite Scores for Students with 2.0 to 2.49 GPAs
23 Percent of Students in CPS
9 Percent of Students Nationally

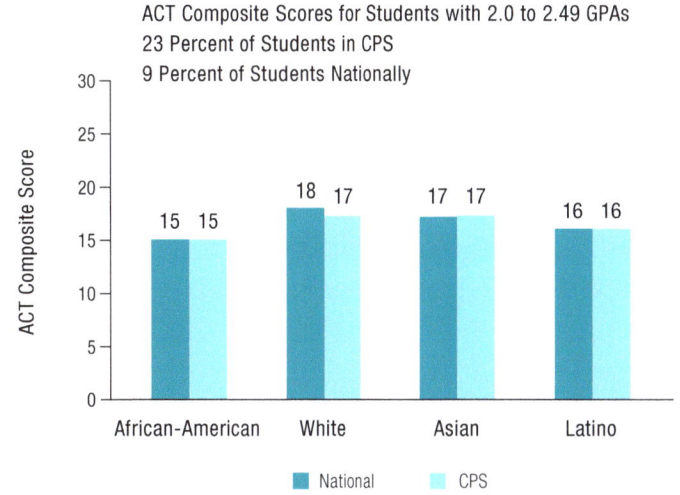

ACT scores by GPA and race/ethnicity: National statistics and CPS

ACT Composite Scores for Students with 3.0 to 3.49 GPAs
16 Percent of Students in CPS
29 Percent of Students Nationally

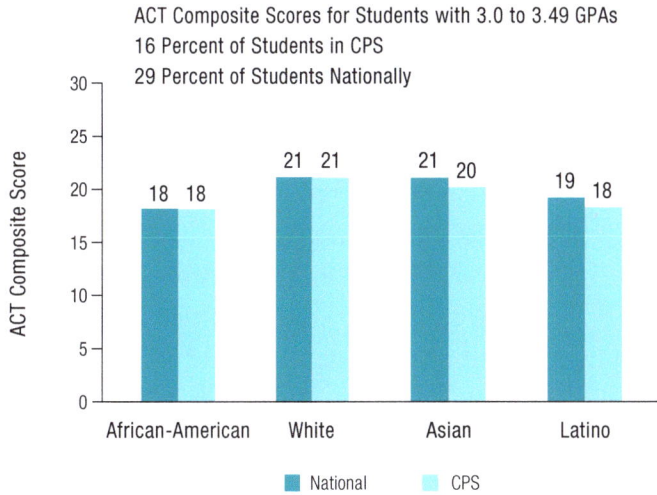

ACT scores by GPA and race/ethnicity: National statistics and CPS

ACT Composite Scores for Students with 1.99 and Below GPAs
25 Percent of Students in CPS
3 Percent of Students Nationally

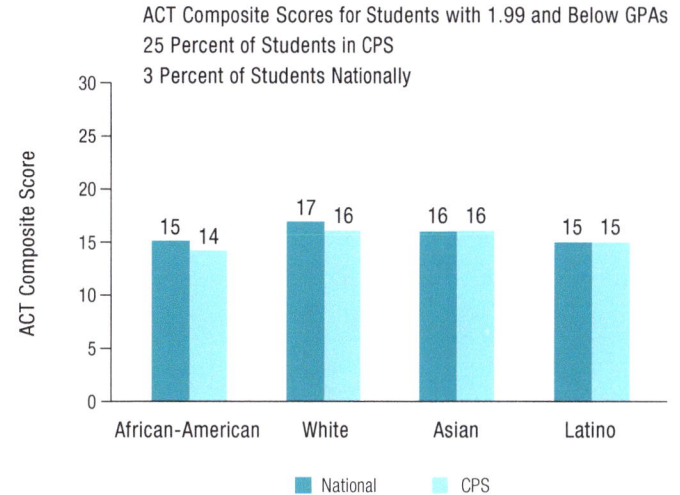

ACT scores by GPA and race/ethnicity: National statistics and CPS

ACT Composite Scores for Students with 2.5 to 2.99 GPAs
18 Percent of Students in CPS
18 Percent of Students Nationally

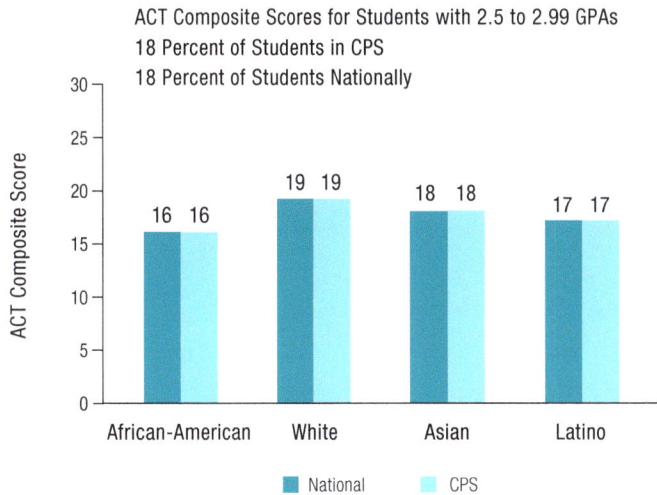

Chapter 1   19

ACT Scores by College Retention

Comparing ACT scores to students' high school grades provides an indirect assessment of whether CPS students' ACT scores accurately reflect their preparation for college. A more direct test would be to compare the college retention and graduation rates for CPS students to students nationally with similar ACT scores. Unfortunately, national data on graduation rates by ACT score are not available. However, ACT has published research on college retention rates in public four-year institutions for students meeting benchmark scores.[25] Among students in the ACT study meeting English, and math benchmarks, 80 percent remained in college after the first year; students meeting English, math and science benchmarks had an 83 percent retention rate. We can compare these retention rates to the retention rates of CPS students who enrolled in four-year colleges by their ACT scores. The CPS Department of Postsecondary Education and Student Development has published college retention rates by students' ACT scores. Their report shows that CPS students receiving an ACT score of 21 or better—who likely met both the English and math benchmarks—have a one-year college retention rate of 81 percent.[26] This is very close to the national one-year retention rates and further suggests that CPS students' ACT scores are indicative of their likely success in college.

In summary, ACT scores are low because many CPS students are not developing the skills they will need, based on comparisons to their course grades and college retention rates. ACT scores in CPS are consistent with poor performance in high school classes.

Are ACT Scores Low Because Students Are Unmotivated for the Test?

When discussing low performance on the ACT, a frequently asked question is whether students are really trying hard on the test. Are they motivated to do the work they will need to prepare for the test? Interviews and the survey data show that they are very motivated. Incorporating the ACT into the state assessment has been very successful at motivating students to work hard to prepare for the test and try to achieve high scores.

Schools are actively working to motivate students for the ACT, and the students are responding positively. Many schools hold motivational assemblies to remind students of the ACT's significance for college admissions and scholarships, and to provide tips for taking the test. Some schools offer rewards and prizes for good performance. Some even design catchy slogans encouraging high achievement and effort. Conversations about the ACT reverberate throughout the entire school from the principals, teachers, counselors, and students.

In What Ways Are Students Under-Performing on the ACT?

On average, CPS students' ACT scores are low compared to the national average. But to what degree are students "under-performing" relative to the scores we would expect them to have? The term under-performance is generally used to describe racial/ethnic disparities in test scores, implying that minority students receive scores that underestimate their true ability. This type of under-performance might result from bias in test design or from such psychological factors as anxiety on the test due to stereotype threat. We do not see evidence of this—students' ACT scores are about where we would expect given their high school course grades and their college retention rates.

However, we might consider broadening the definition of under-performance. CPS students' scores are low given their aspirations for college. Average ACT scores fall beneath students' own expectations for their test performance, expectations that were based on college goals. Their ACT scores are also under what we would expect given their performance on tests in earlier grades. CPS students' test scores are not keeping up with those of students nationally as they move through high school. **CPS students are under-performing in that they are not getting the skills they will need to meet their college aspirations, even though most seemed like they were ready in earlier years.**

FIGURE 7

Almost all students agree it is important to do well on PSAE

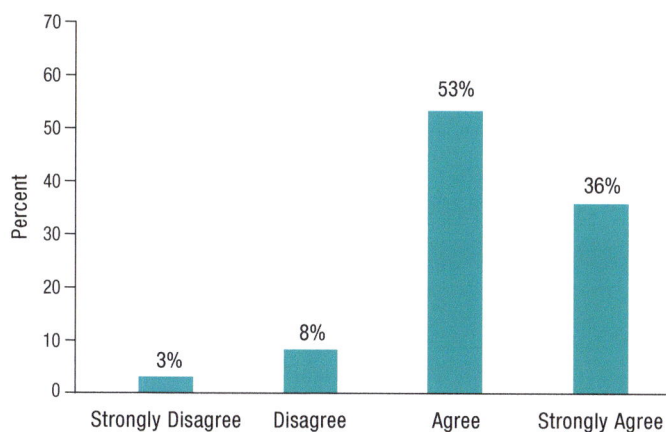

Note: These statistics are based on 11th grade students surveyed in spring 2005.

"They pull them out to have an assembly to tell them how serious they should take the test. They talk to them for like 40 minutes about how they need to do well on the test, eat a good meal beforehand."—Teacher

Students have embraced the message. In 2005, the CCSR citywide survey asked juniors how important it was for them to "do well" on the PSAE (which includes the ACT). They overwhelmingly agreed that it was important—89 percent of juniors endorsed this statement (see Figure 7). When the survey was repeated in 2007 and we asked this question again, 90 percent of juniors agreed that it was important to do well.[27]

"I want to be known as a kid who had a good score, . . . because I'm not an average person. I don't feel like I'm an average person, so why get an average score? Get a high score."—Student

"We taught this ACT prep course at the school.... I had students just coming in there...because they wanted to do well on the ACT, even though they weren't really involved in the [regular] class."—Teacher

Almost all students we interviewed said it was important to them to do well on the ACT. The real-life consequences for college scholarships are highly motivating to students, as is the ACT press in school. Even students who were not planning on going to college

said they wanted to do well because they thought the test was a reflection of their abilities. The majority of students take the test very seriously, even if they are not normally high-achieving students.

Are ACT Scores Low Because Students Spend Insufficient Time Preparing for the Test?

Both our interviews and our survey data suggest that, in fact, CPS students spend extraordinary amounts of time preparing for the ACT. As one student put it, "Junior year's really about prepping for the ACTs."

"These teachers really want us to do well on the ACT, so every single class that we have, every single teacher . . . was making us do ACT work at least twice a week. [Mr. X] took us every week for . . . [Work Keys], and every Monday he actually made us read passages,... answer questions, and [Miss C] made us do science ACT every Tuesday, and [Miss G] she made us do a couple of pages every day . . . and British Lit, I think that's the class we did ACT the most because I think there is a part that involves reading, and basically we did like five days of ACT straight."—Eleventh-grade student

"When I first started, the ACT test was given outside of class. It was given on weekends. . . . Now, you put your whole entire curriculum on hold. I mean, you just throw it out the window and you do nothing but test preparation the whole entire period for weeks. You know, five, six, seven, eight weeks leading up to the test."—Eleventh-grade teacher

Students are spending much of the eleventh grade preparing for the ACT, particularly within their regular academic classes. We found this through our interviews in the field work schools and systemwide in the surveys. The 2005 survey asked teachers how much class time would be spent having students practice for standardized tests (see Figure 8). English teachers were the most likely to engage in test preparation; almost 60 percent of eleventh-grade English teachers spent more than 20 hours practicing for standardized tests. This translates to at least one month

Are Work Keys Scores Lower Than ACT Scores in CPS?

There is both local and statewide concern that students are not trying hard enough on the Work Keys portion of the PSAE. While ACT scores improved slightly from 2006 to 2007, Work Keys scores went down slightly.[28] In interviews, students were clearly less concerned about their performance on the second day of the PSAE (testing the non-ACT components) than on the ACT, which is given on the first day. When talking about how they did on the test, most students considered the Work Keys section of the test to be much easier. This might suggest that students were not trying as hard. However, an analysis of students' scores suggests that the lack of concern about Work Keys scores is not resulting in substantial under-performance on the second day of the test.

Work Keys performance in CPS corresponds closely with performance on the main part of the ACT. There is a very strong correspondence between students' ACT scores and Work Keys scores. Almost all students with weak Work Keys scores have low ACT scores.[29] ACT says that a Work Keys reading score of 5 is comparable to an ACT reading score of 19–23, while a Work Keys math score of 5 is comparable to an ACT math score of 18–21.[30] Among CPS students with ACT scores of 20 in reading or math in 2007, half scored a 5 on the Work Keys, while about a quarter scored a 4, and a quarter scored a 6. In other words, it was most common for students to receive the Work Keys score that was expected given their ACT score; almost all of those students who did not receive the expected score were at the level immediately below or above their expected score.

of instructional time. For math and science teachers, 40 percent spent at least one month of instructional time on test preparation, and an additional quarter spent 13 to 20 hours on test preparation, which is three to four weeks.

In the 2007 survey, we asked more specific questions about what teachers were doing to prepare for the standardized tests. Figure 9 shows the responses of eleventh-grade English, math, and science teachers to questions about how often during the spring term their students used class time for Work Keys practice, learning test-taking strategies, going through practice test answers, or taking timed tests. Learning and practicing test-taking strategies was the most common method of preparing for the ACT, closely followed by going through answers on practice tests. More than half of eleventh-grade teachers did these at least weekly, and more than 80 percent did them at least once a month. The vast majority of teachers (almost 70 percent) also used class time for Work Keys practice and taking timed tests at least once a month, and about half did Work Keys practice and timed tests at least once a week. We also asked teachers about how much time they had spent in their class having students practice

taking standardized tests and learning test-taking skills since January (see Figure 10). One-fifth of core subject teachers (English, math, and science) reported spending more than half of their class time in the spring on test preparation. Half of core subject teachers spent 30 percent or more of class time practicing test-taking and learning test-taking skills.

> "When the school purchased a study packet from Kaplan, we were required to do it. I think it was two days a week. Two full class periods a week, for eight weeks. Most often the lessons were more confusing than helpful to a lot of the students."—Teacher

Many schools have mandated that teachers spend time preparing for the PSAE, although they have done so in different ways. In our field work sample, one school started at the very beginning of the year, when students received their scores back from the fall PLAN exam. Another school concentrated heavily on preparation close to the test date. One school allocated a set number of days per week for test preparation. Some schools have classes for juniors devoted to preparing for the PSAE or ACT. On our

2007 systemwide survey, more than three-fourths of all eleventh-grade teachers—including 90 percent of eleventh-grade math teachers and 84 percent of eleventh-grade science teachers—reported that they were required by their school to spend class time on practice tests and test-taking skills. Furthermore, in the schools where we did field work, it was not just eleventh-grade teachers who said they were required to spend class time preparing their students for the PSAE, but teachers with any eleventh-graders in their class. Even if their class predominantly consisted of seniors, who had already taken the PSAE, some teachers reported that they were required to spend class time on PSAE preparation.

Teachers spent large amounts of class time on test preparation not only because of pressure from administration, but also because they want their students to do well on the exam. They want to make sure their students have access to college and scholarships. They also want their school to look good on accountability measures. Thus, when the school asks them to spend time on preparation for the ACT, they are likely to comply.

> "They will need good ACT scores in order to have the pick of the best colleges. And if I can help them improve their test scores then that's great."—Eleventh-grade teacher

In addition to preparation during classes, many students spend time outside of class preparing for the ACT. All of the field work schools offered ACT preparation classes for students, usually held after school. Some students mentioned that their parents bought them ACT guidebooks or computer programs so that they could study for the ACT on their own. Even the students getting the least amount of test preparation in their classes, typically students in the AP/IB tracks, still reported working on test preparation for homework. However, most test preparation occurred during students' class time. Half of juniors prepare for the ACT in class every day or almost every day in the month before the exam (see Figure 11). Given that so much class time is spent on test preparation, students might not feel as pressed to prepare on their own. However, more than half still reported preparing for the ACT on their own at least

FIGURE 8

Teachers commonly spend a month of instructional time on ACT practice during eleventh grade core classes

In an average class, how much class time will be spent having students practice for standardized tests this year?

Eleventh Grade Teachers

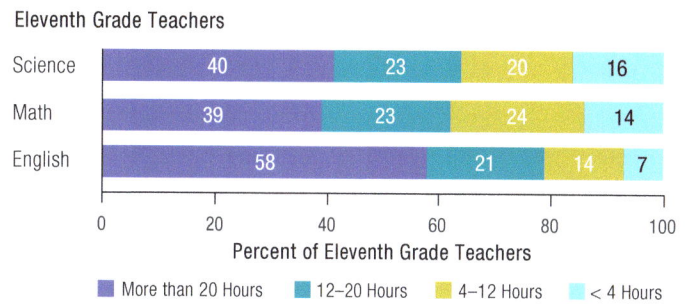

Legend: More than 20 Hours | 12–20 Hours | 4–12 Hours | < 4 Hours

Note: These statistics are based on 11th grade teachers surveyed in 2005.

FIGURE 9

Most eleventh grade teachers regularly do Work Keys and ACT practice and teach testing strategies

How often did your students do the following during class time in the spring term?

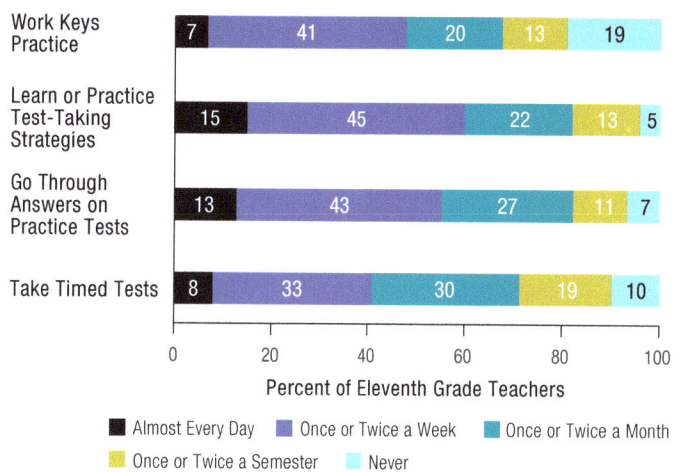

Legend: Almost Every Day | Once or Twice a Week | Once or Twice a Month | Once or Twice a Semester | Never

Note: These frequencies are based on 11th grade math, English and science teachers surveyed in spring 2007.

FIGURE 10

Half of core-subject teachers spend at least 30 percent of class time on test practice beginning in January

Since January, how much time have you spent in class having students practice taking standardized tests and learning test-taking skills?

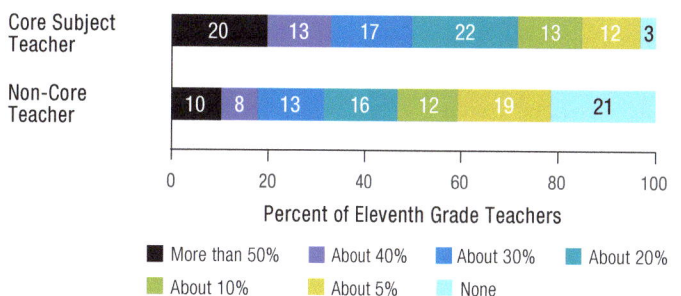

Legend: More than 50% | About 40% | About 30% | About 20% | About 10% | About 5% | None

Note: These percentages are based on 11th grade teachers surveyed in spring 2007.

Prior Research on the Effects of Test Preparation on ACT Scores

There is little evidence from previous research that time spent on test practice and testing strategies benefits students' ACT scores. The few studies that exist on the effects of test practice, coaching, and strategies find no more than minimal positive effects and often find no effects or negative effects. For example, one study showed that one-on-one coaching had an effect of raising ACT math scores by between 0 and 0.4 points and English scores by between 0.3 and 0.6 points; in reading, the effect of coaching on ACT scores was negative by 0.6 to 0.7 points.[31] A study by ACT researchers found that only one test preparation activity—taking practice tests—was associated with higher ACT scores, but only by an average of 0.4 points. These authors found that workbooks and test preparation courses produced slightly lower scores (by 0.6 points).[32] As we show in the next chapter, the more that schools emphasize test preparation in class, the lower are their students' ACT scores, even after adjusting for students' initial scores, their background characteristics, teacher characteristics, and school characteristics.

It may seem counterintuitive that learning test strategies and practicing items would hurt students' scores. However, there are a number of potential reasons these approaches do not work. We see from our surveys of students that many think the ACT tests their test-taking skills (see Figure 16 on page 31). With this perspective, they may work less hard on solving the problems in their attempts to figure out the solution based on test strategies. Their concern with following strategies may also distract students from simply trying to solve the problems in the exam. Advice from different testing sources can be contradictory, and this may make the exam more confusing.[33] Going through test items question by question during practice may give students a false sense of pacing or may lead them to develop strategies that are not effective under timed conditions. In general, the ACT is designed not to be influenced by test preparation and strategies.

FIGURE 11

About half of eleventh graders prepare for the ACT in their classes almost every day; many prepare on their own almost every day

During the month before the ACT, how often did you...

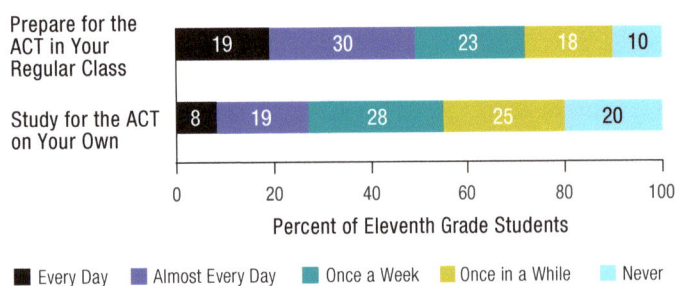

	Every Day	Almost Every Day	Once a Week	Once in a While	Never
Prepare for the ACT in Your Regular Class	19	30	23	18	10
Study for the ACT on Your Own	8	19	28	25	20

Percent of Eleventh Grade Students

Note: These frequencies are based on 11th grade students surveyed in spring 2007.

once a week during the month before the exam; a quarter said they prepared on their own almost every day.

The students we interviewed seemed to value all sources of test preparation, regardless of their source or content, because they were so motivated to do well on the test. They often reported that they did not enjoy it, but they said it was useful and necessary. The few exceptions to this general acceptance of test preparation were among low-achieving students, who tended to spend extremely large amounts of class time doing test preparation. While these students were still positive about the need to do test preparation, many did feel that the amount of time spent on it was excessive.

Even practice on the Work Keys portion of the PSAE was viewed by some students as a good use of time. Most students did not care about doing well on the non-ACT portions of the test, but in some schools that emphasized Work Keys, students mistakenly thought Work Keys practice would help their ACT score. Thus, even preparation for other sections of the test often was viewed positively by students because they were so anxious to score well on the ACT.

A Closer Look at ACT Scores by Race and Ethnicity

Racial/ethnic differences in ACT scores are disturbingly large. This is troubling not only because it suggests unequal education in high school, but also because it implies very unequal chances for attaining a college degree. Gaps in test scores are large even when we compare students with similar grades in high school, and this suggests another cause for concern—why should students graded by their teachers as having similar high school course performance score so differently on the test used for high school accountability in Illinois? Is this a fair test for high schools that predominantly serve racial/ethnic minority students? Here we look at some of the factors behind these large racial/ethnic gaps in performance.

Is the ACT Racially Biased?

A number of studies have looked at whether college entrance exam scores (the ACT or the SAT) under-predict the college performance of racial/ethnic minority students to determine whether the test is biased against them. These studies consistently find no evidence of under-prediction.[34] However, while the ACT does not under-predict students' success in college based on race/ethnicity, it still might be biased as an indicator of high school learning. High school and college teachers often disagree about the skills students need, and, where there is disagreement, the ACT emphasizes skills emphasized by college teachers.[35] If the ACT tests skills needed for college that are learned at home to a greater degree than at school, this could lead racial/ethnic minority students to have lower scores than white students. For example, the ACT tests students' familiarity with standard English and ability to understand complex, technical vocabulary. These skills—which are needed in college—may be learned to a larger degree in students' homes than at school. If they are not emphasized in high school classes, the scores will not be a good representation of classroom learning. ACT, Inc., has produced a report that concludes race is only slightly associated with test performance, once noncognitive skills and high school course work are taken into account.[36] However, a close look at their analysis suggests race and home culture effects.[37]

Since the ACT is being used for school accountability in Illinois and in other states, such bias could unfairly hurt schools that serve large numbers of racial/ethnic minority students. As we show below, we also continue to see racial/ethnic differences in ACT scores among students in Chicago once we compare students with similar grades, academic programs, and schools—particularly among students with high grades. The differences are modest—less than one point—but they are persistent.

Reasons behind the Racial Gaps among CPS Students

The main reason there are large racial/ethnic gaps in eleventh-grade ACT scores among CPS students with similar GPAs is that there are large racial/ethnic gaps in skill levels when students enter high school. While it might seem that students with the same course grades should demonstrate the same academic skills, we must remember that grades do not just reflect an absolute level of learning in a class; they also reflect the progress that students have made in that class and the effort they have put into their work.[38] Students who enter a class with low test scores may work hard and show substantial progress, yet a sizable gain in test scores could still leave them with a lower score than other students who gained less but started out with stronger skills. This seems to be the case in CPS—once we control for students' prior test scores, the racial gaps in ACT performance among students with similar grades shrink to about a quarter of their original size (see Figure 12). The differences are particularly large among students with A averages (GPAs of 3.5 or higher). Many Latino and African American students are working hard and earning As in their classes, but because they started so far behind their white and Asian peers in academic skills, their ACT scores remain several points lower.

FIGURE 12

Racial/ethnic gaps in ACT scores among students with similar grades are largely explained by incoming skills

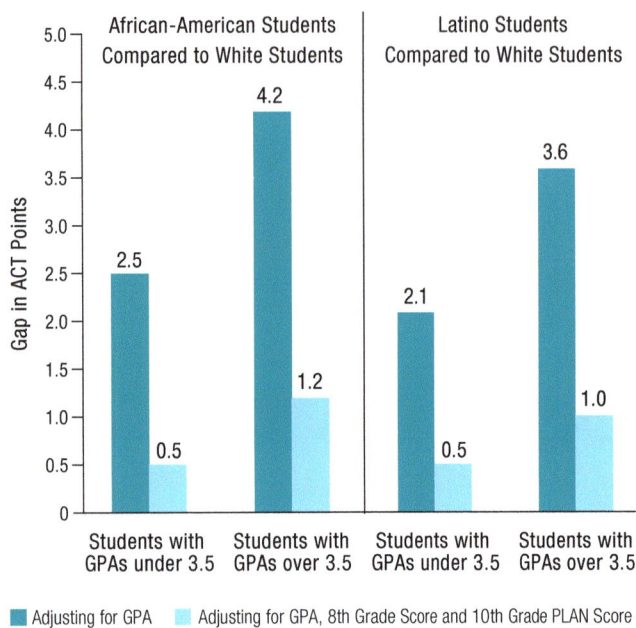

Note: Differences are shown for students with GPAs under 3.5 and over 3.5, but adjustments for grades took into account all levels of GPA. For example, the gap shown for students with GPAs under 3.5 takes into account that some students had GPAs of 1, others 1.5, others 2.0, etc. We show the gap separately for students with high GPAs because the racial differences in ACT scores are largest among students with B+ averages or better.

Large racial gaps in academic preparation prior to high school are a great concern. Figure 13 shows the average EXPLORE, PLAN, and ACT scores for students who took all three tests, separated by students' race/ethnicity. African American students start off high school with test scores that are, on average, about four points lower than those of white and Asian students, while Latino students are three points behind, on average. The average African American student who takes the ACT in CPS had an EXPLORE score of 14 in reading and math when the student was in ninth grade. To make the benchmark scores on the ACT, the student would have to show improvements of seven points in reading and eight points in math. Yet, the average improvement for students scoring a 14 on the EXPLORE is just two points in math and three points in reading. Thus, most African American students in CPS had virtually no chance of making the ACT benchmark scores unless they made remarkable gains in learning while in high school.

Besides starting off with much lower test scores in ninth grade, African American and Latino students also showed smaller improvements in test scores from the ninth-grade EXPLORE to the eleventh-grade ACT than did white or Asian students. As shown in Figure 13, the average Asian or white student scored four points higher on the ACT than the EXPLORE. Yet, the typical African American and Latino student scored only two points higher on the ACT than the EXPLORE.

We further break down the reasons behind the black-white gap in ACT scores by looking simultaneously at a number of factors that might contribute to differences in test performance. Figure 14 graphs the gap in ACT scores between white and African American students that remains after we take out differences that can be explained by students' backgrounds and course performance. Each subject test is graphed separately. The first bar in each set shows the average gap across all students—the black-white gap ranges from three points in science to almost four points in math. The next bar takes out those differences that can be explained by students' economic status—the gap is slightly smaller, but large differences by race remain across students with similar economic backgrounds who live in economically similar neighborhoods.[39]

The biggest reduction in the racial gap occurs when we take into account students' eighth-grade test scores—African American students are entering high schools with much lower levels of academic skills than white students. Students' eighth-grade achievement explains more than half of the racial gap in ACT scores. Not only do low levels of incoming achievement make it hard for students to reach ACT benchmarks, but students' achievement in elementary school also affects their likelihood of getting into high-achieving high schools. Therefore, some of the effects of incoming achievement could also be due to school effects, with higher-achieving students attending higher-achieving high schools and vice versa. The high school that students attend affects their ACT score—the next bar removes the differences in ACT scores that can be explained by the school that students attend and their

FIGURE 13

Racial gaps in EPAS scores begin before ninth grade, grow larger after high school

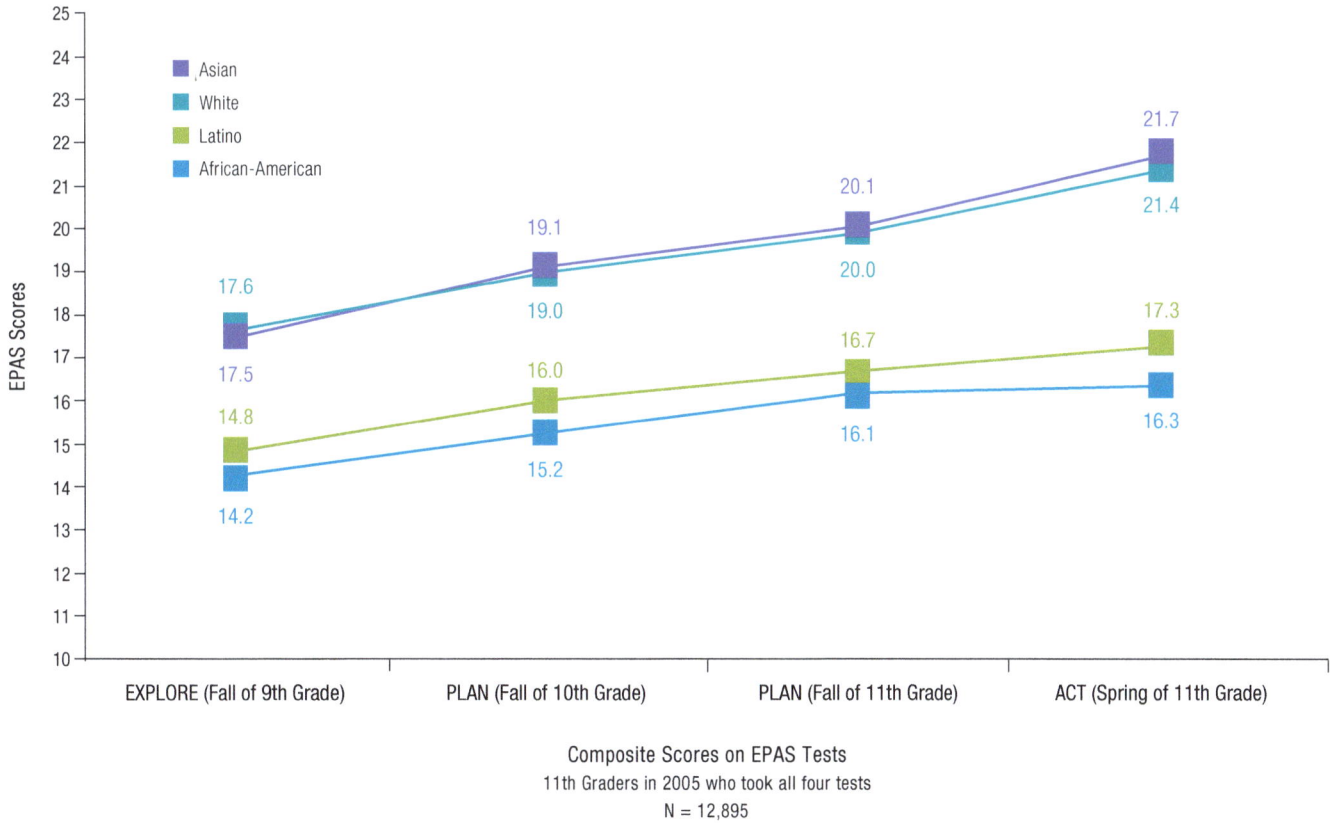

Asian
White
Latino
African-American

17.6
17.5
14.8
14.2

19.1
19.0
16.0
15.2

20.1
20.0
16.7
16.1

21.7
21.4
17.3
16.3

EPAS Scores

EXPLORE (Fall of 9th Grade)   PLAN (Fall of 10th Grade)   PLAN (Fall of 11th Grade)   ACT (Spring of 11th Grade)

Composite Scores on EPAS Tests
11th Graders in 2005 who took all four tests
N = 12,895

FIGURE 14

Racial gaps are mostly explained by differences in students' preparation prior to high school, but enrollment patterns in different high schools and curricular tracks widen the gap

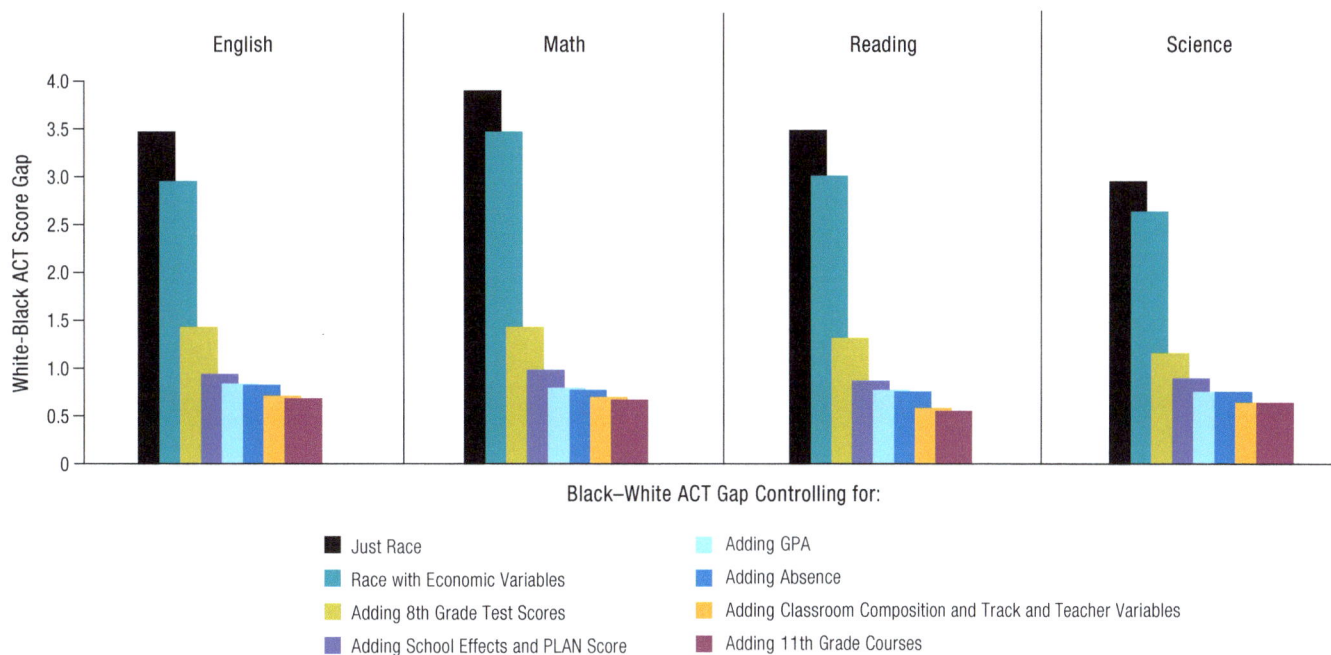

English   Math   Reading   Science

White-Black ACT Score Gap

Black–White ACT Gap Controlling for:

■ Just Race
■ Race with Economic Variables
■ Adding 8th Grade Test Scores
■ Adding School Effects and PLAN Score
■ Adding GPA
■ Adding Absence
■ Adding Classroom Composition and Track and Teacher Variables
■ Adding 11th Grade Courses

achievement on the tenth-grade test.

White students are more likely to go to selective enrollment schools with high-achieving peers, and they average higher improvements on tests during their freshman year. These differences affect their ACT scores by about half a point beyond their incoming achievement levels. White students get higher grades, on average, than African American students, and this also explains some of the gap. Attendance doesn't explain the gap beyond its relationship with course grades. White students are more likely to be in higher-track classes with high-ability peers, and this further explains some of the racial gap. Once we take into account students' academic track, their grades and their earlier test scores, the type of class they took in eleventh grade (e.g., Algebra 2 vs. Geometry vs. Precalculus) doesn't further explain the gap in ACT scores. Because course selection is so strongly associated with the other explanatory variables, these effects might already be taken into account by the earlier factors. Thus, the racial gaps are mostly explained by differences in students' preparation prior to high school, but enrollment patterns in different high schools and curricular tracks widen the gap. While not shown, similar patterns can be seen in the Latino-white gap in ACT scores.

Chapter 2

Are Students' Test Preparation Efforts Effective for Raising Their Scores?

If CPS students are highly motivated to do well on the ACT and spending so much time preparing for the ACT, why are improvements from the PLAN to the ACT below national averages? Is the way they are preparing for the test not helping them succeed? We begin to answer these questions by looking at what students say they are doing to prepare for the exam. We then compare students' descriptions of test preparation to those of teachers, and then consider these descriptions in relation to the content of the ACT itself and their scores on the test.

Test Preparation Is Mostly Work on Sample Problems and Test Strategies

Regardless of the source of the test preparation—in their academic courses, at home, in test preparation classes—students generally characterize test preparation as doing sample test items. Much of this work involves learning test-taking strategies, like skimming reading passages, moving ahead, and process of elimination. Teachers also acknowledge spending substantial time having students practice these strategies.

It was rare for students we interviewed to mention specific academic skills that they needed to work on for the ACT. There was no indication that students were taking control of their subject matter learning in preparation for the ACT. For example, students rarely pointed out weaknesses in English or math skills, such as adding and subtracting equations. When they did mention specific academic skills, it was to acknowledge that they lacked certain skills, rather than to say that they were working on them. For example, two students recognized that they were poor readers, but their strategy for improvement was vague—in the week before the exam they planned on doing a lot of reading. A number of students talked about going over geometry or formulas in their math classes, but not understanding how to do them:

> "I know I'm not prepared. Last year in geometry I didn't pay too much attention, and I wish I would have now because I would just sit there like, wow, I don't know this stuff."—Student talking about geometry review in eleventh-grade math

The 2007 survey also showed that many students spend a great deal of time taking practice tests (see Figure 15). They are also likely to spend time going through practice test answers and review strategies for eliminating answers. Grammar reviews are common for the English subject test, and skill reviews are common in math class, although subject matter content review occurs less frequently than taking practice tests.

Students and Teachers Believe ACT Scores Are Largely Determined by Test-Taking Skills

The emphasis on test-taking practice corresponds with students' views about what matters for doing well on the test. Most students believe that ACT scores are strongly determined by tenacity and practice. When students were asked in interviews what they were doing to prepare for the test, the most common response was that they were going to try hard. In the 2007 survey, more than 80 percent of students said that ACT scores are largely a reflection of test-taking skills; this was far higher than the proportion of students who believed that ACT scores reflect high school learning or college preparation (see Figure 16). Students were least likely to agree that the ACT reflects how well they will do in college. Yet, the ACT is primarily designed to predict college performance.

Student perceptions that tenacity, strategies, and practice are what matter most for test scores are

reinforced by the large amount of class time spent on practice items, strategies, pep assemblies around the test, and motivational posters. Commercial practice guides also encourage this perception. The Kaplan ACT guide states, "The answer to every ACT question can be found in the test. Theoretically, if you read carefully and understand the words and concepts the test

FIGURE 15

Most students report doing both skill review and test practice

How much did you do the following when preparing for the ACT Math section?

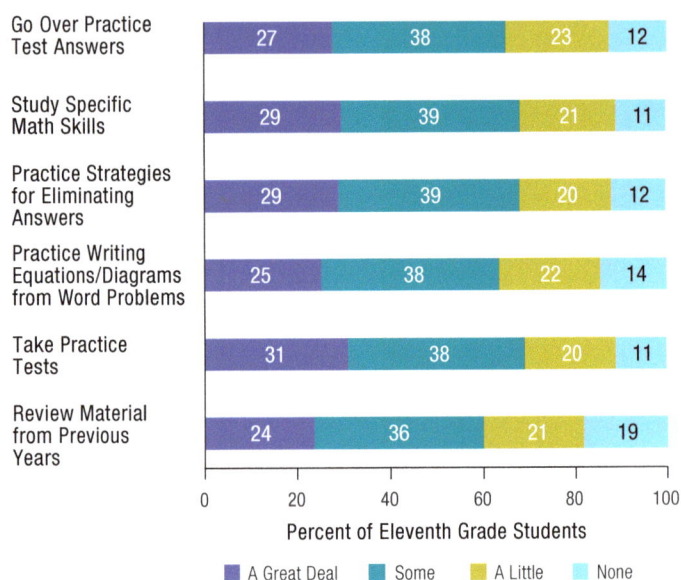

Percent of Eleventh Grade Students

■ A Great Deal ■ Some ■ A Little ■ None

How much did you do the following when preparing for the ACT Reading and English sections?

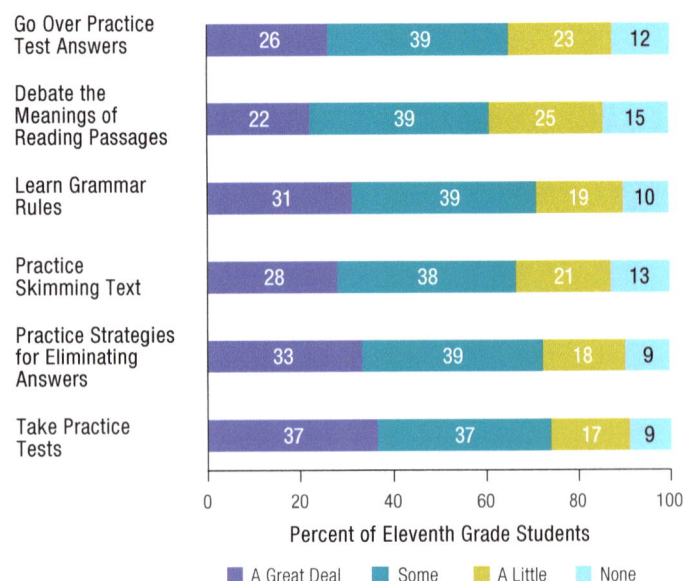

Percent of Eleventh Grade Students

■ A Great Deal ■ Some ■ A Little ■ None

Note: These frequencies are based on 11th grade students surveyed in spring 2007.

FIGURE 16

Students believe ACT scores reflect test-taking skills more than academic strengths

How much do you agree with the following about the ACT/PSAE?

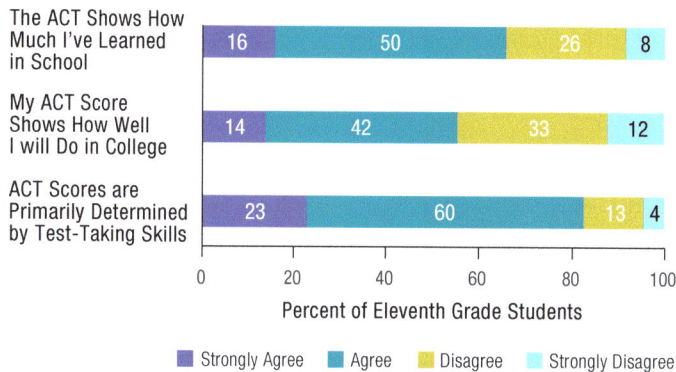

	Strongly Agree	Agree	Disagree	Strongly Disagree
The ACT Shows How Much I've Learned in School	16	50	26	8
My ACT Score Shows How Well I will Do in College	14	42	33	12
ACT Scores are Primarily Determined by Test-Taking Skills	23	60	13	4

Percent of Eleventh Grade Students

■ Strongly Agree ■ Agree ■ Disagree ■ Strongly Disagree

Note: These frequencies are based on 11th grade students surveyed in spring 2007.

FIGURE 17

Teachers believe ACT scores demonstrate test-taking skills more than student learning in high school

The ACT and PLAN are good measures of student learning in high school

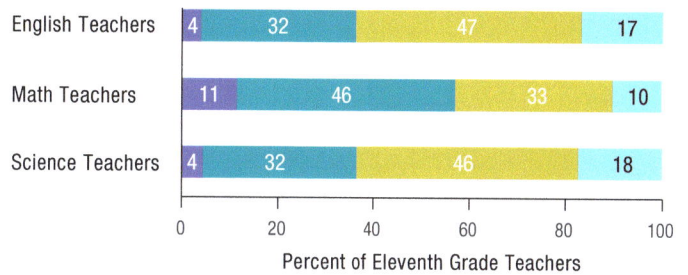

	Strongly Agree	Agree	Disagree	Strongly Disagree
English Teachers	4	32	47	17
Math Teachers	11	46	33	10
Science Teachers	4	32	46	18

Percent of Eleventh Grade Teachers

The ACT and PLAN are good measures of what students need to know for college

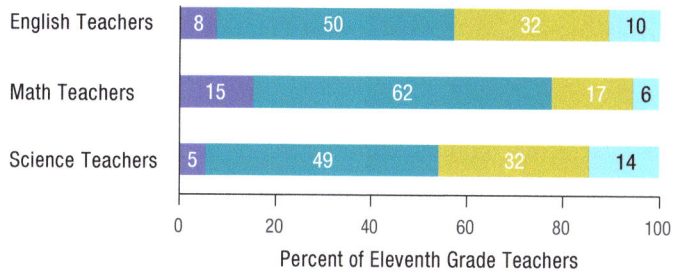

	Strongly Agree	Agree	Disagree	Strongly Disagree
English Teachers	8	50	32	10
Math Teachers	15	62	17	6
Science Teachers	5	49	32	14

Percent of Eleventh Grade Teachers

Students scores are mostly determined by test-taking skills

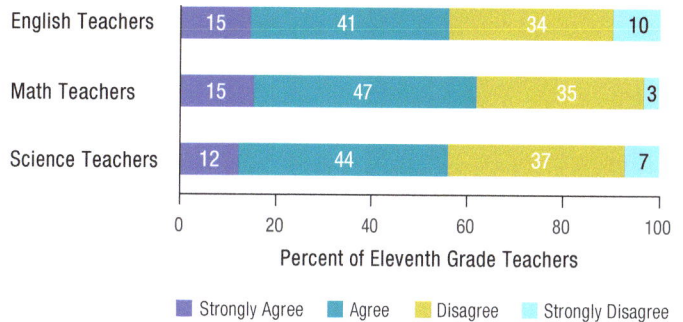

	Strongly Agree	Agree	Disagree	Strongly Disagree
English Teachers	15	41	34	10
Math Teachers	15	47	35	3
Science Teachers	12	44	37	7

Percent of Eleventh Grade Teachers

■ Strongly Agree ■ Agree ■ Disagree ■ Strongly Disagree

Note: These frequencies are based on 11th grade teachers surveyed in spring 2007.

uses, you can get almost every ACT question right."[40] It also states that the ACT is "highly vulnerable to test-smart strategies and techniques." In other words, by becoming test-savvy one can get a top score. Given what students are hearing from sources providing them test practice, it is not surprising that many think ACT scores are based largely on desire and test-taking skills and strategies.

Teachers also tend to believe that ACT scores are predominantly determined by test-taking skills—almost 60 percent believe so (see Figure 17). More teachers believe that the ACT reflects testing skills than believe it reflects student learning in their classes. Belief in the importance of test-taking skills may encourage teachers to spend time on practice tests and testing strategies in their classes. Among students, this belief might suggest that they should spend their effort more on testing practice and tricks than on substantive work related to their courses. As we will discuss below, test-taking skills and practice are not good strategies for improving ACT scores. Furthermore, there is evidence that students and teachers are not using practice tests correctly, and this misuse may be hurting student performance.

Misuse and Misperceptions of Practice ACT Tests Are Common

As we will show later in this report, there are limits to how much test practice can raise students' scores.

Beyond this limitation, many teachers and students are not using and interpreting practice tests in intended ways: many tests used for practice are not actually ACT practice tests; often there is no time element in practice; and there are misperceptions about how students should interpret their practice test scores.

The following quote from an eleventh-grade teacher provides an example of some of the key problems with the way practice tests are used. The teacher talks about a practice test given in the fall of the junior year, with scores returned around October with a test booklet. This description exactly matches the district implementation of the PLAN exam; yet, the teacher does not recognize the difference between the PLAN given to juniors in the fall and an actual practice ACT exam. Furthermore, she is going through PLAN during class at an extremely slow pace—one or two passages per period:

> "It's mandated that we spend one day a week, starting at the beginning . . . probably around October. Because they took a practice test and we got the results back, and they got their test booklet. So we went over that, and it usually took us one period to do one or two passages. So we read probably like five passages, so it took us maybe like six weeks to do it all."—Eleventh-grade teacher

The teacher quoted above is far from alone. In interview after interview, we found that it was common for both teachers and students to refer to the PLAN as the practice ACT. CPS bought the EPAS system as preparation for the ACT, and ACT itself describes the PLAN as a "pre-ACT" in their marketing materials.[41] ACT provides summary reports from the PLAN of skills students will need in preparation for the actual ACT. Thus, it makes sense that schools would describe the PLAN as a practice ACT when motivating students to take it, and teachers would use it as practice for the ACT.

However, the ACT is 50 percent longer than the PLAN and is a more difficult exam (see Table 4). The length makes it much more grueling for students to sit through. The content is quite different; the PLAN tests tenth-grade skills, while the ACT tests twelfth-grade skills. For example, the math portion of the PLAN only tests knowledge of pre-algebra, first-year algebra, and plane geometry—mostly topics covered before the second year of high school[42]—yet the ACT also covers advanced algebra, trigonometry, and coordinate geometry.[43] The complexity and difficulty of

questions in all subjects is much higher on the ACT. (See "Comparing the PLAN to the ACT" on page 33 for further discussion.) Students and teachers who only use the PLAN to gauge students' skill levels to prepare for the ACT will overestimate their preparation.

Students were caught off guard when they took the actual ACT and faced more difficult questions than they did while "practicing." Many expressed dismay with time on the test and reported they were unable to finish. The surprise expressed by so many students about the length and difficulty of the ACT is startling, given the extent of test preparation they received.

> "It was hard. I thought it would be a little easier because of the practice test that we had taken before. And on those practice tests, I had gotten like a composite score of probably like 30 or something like that, but that was because it was the sophomore test."—Student

> Interviewer: Did you do about the same as you did on the practice tests or different?
> Student: The problems on the actual tests to me looked way more complicated than the practice tests. But I don't know. They caught me off guard.

There are also misconceptions about the relationships between PLAN and ACT scores. There is a pervasive belief among students, teachers, and administrators that test scores increase by two points between the PLAN and the ACT. Students did not know why their scores were expected to improve. Misunderstandings about scores on these tests cause students to be misguided in their expectations about their ACT scores and lead students to believe they are more prepared than they actually are.

That scores increase by two points between tests is a myth for a variety of reasons. It is true that the average improvement between the PLAN and ACT in national samples is two points for students with some PLAN scores; however, the average improvement is only one point for students with some other PLAN scores.[44] Beyond this, on average, CPS students show smaller improvements from the PLAN to the ACT than the national samples. Most importantly, the

TABLE 4

Number of questions in the PLAN and ACT exams

	Math	English	Reading	Science
PLAN	40 items	50	25	30
ACT	60 items	75	40	40

Comparing the PLAN to the ACT

The ACT questions require much more analysis, judgment, and attention to detail than questions in the PLAN, particularly in the science, reading, and math subject tests. Consider, for example, the first set of questions in the science portion of a practice PLAN and a practice ACT (see pages 64-70). The PLAN questions are about a topic very familiar in the everyday lives of students—weather. To answer these questions, students read a chart on weather conditions in different cities and apply the information in the chart to straightforward questions, essentially showing that they can read a bar graph. In contrast, the ACT questions are about plasmids found in bacteria—a topic that is unfamiliar to most people. The ACT questions refer to a diagram, but the questions cannot be answered simply by looking at the diagram. Instead, students have to consider the information given in the text and use that information to interpret the diagram. For example, Question 2 asks students to interpret the diagram based on the theory proposed by a student in a science class. Thus, to answer the ACT questions, students need to be able to incorporate unfamiliar vocabulary and concepts, and go through multiple steps to discern the correct answer.

The questions in the PLAN reading subject test often can be answered simply by finding information in the text targeted by the question. Many questions are answered without much analysis or inference. For example, the first question in the sample passage in Appendix B (page 69) asks why Macon thought he had disappointed Muriel; line 54 directly states that he felt he disappointed her, and the lines immediately before that show him unable to answer her question (one of the response choices). In contrast, the first question about the Eleanor Roosevelt passage in the ACT example (Appendix A, page 66) asks students to figure out how the author is describing Eleanor Roosevelt, using terms that are not directly stated in the text, requiring consideration of the entire passage. Not only is the vocabulary more difficult, but students need to make substantial inferences and consider multiple statements about Eleanor Roosevelt provided throughout the passage. Unlike the PLAN, questions in the ACT reading subject test can rarely be answered by finding a particular section of the reading passage that directly provides the answer. They require the reader to consider statements within a broader context.

The math questions in the PLAN are fairly straightforward problems that require direct application of particular math skills. Some of the math questions in the ACT are similarly straightforward, but most are not. It is often not immediately clear how to solve the problem that is presented, many problems require multiple steps, often they contain long passages of text to set up the math problem, and they require close attention to details. Problem 1 in the sample ACT math items in Appendix A (page 64), for example, is fairly straightforward, but it requires students to spend a long time reading the passage. Problem 16 looks straightforward, but it requires students to revisualize the accompanying figure and then use negative logic to eliminate potential answers (e.g., students are asked whether it is *not* true that AC is about equal to BD—an awkward phrasing that requires students to decipher the question as well as interpret the figure). Contrast that to Problem 4 in the PLAN, which looks similar, but simply requires students to solve for the size of an angle and has a diagram that accurately reflects the conditions stated in the problem. Problem 51 in the ACT is a very long problem—particularly for students who have been told they should spend less than a minute on each problem—but it is not the longest math problem in the sample test. And besides containing a long passage of text, Problem 51 requires students to figure out a method to solve the problem and then apply that method to figure out an answer in a multistep manner. Besides testing more advanced math skills, problems in the ACT are much more demanding than those in the PLAN in their demands on reading, analysis, and attention to detail.

The Tools Teachers Are Using to Prepare Students for the ACT

An abundance of test preparation materials is available to teachers. In interviews, teachers talked about using ACT guides, practice exams (including the PLAN), guides from such commercial companies as Kaplan and Cambridge, and computer software. Some teachers we interviewed said their schools bought commercial packages (e.g., Kaplan) and required their teachers to use them. One teacher bought commercial test-preparation guides on her own for her classes. Teachers at two schools where we conducted interviews noted that their schools had computer software with practice tests available, and at those schools teachers brought their students to the computer lab to use this software. At one of these schools, the computer software was specifically for the Work Keys portion of the PSAE. In addition, some teachers discussed bringing in their own materials to work on specific skills that are tested on the ACT. For example, one Algebra II teacher brought in a book of problems for the class to review geometry, while an English teacher started each week with a quiz on a specific element of grammar tested on the ACT.

Teachers' responses to the 2007 survey confirm the availability of a variety of materials to help prepare their students for the ACT (see Figure 18). Almost 90 percent received practice exams, and about 80 percent received the ACT instructional guides, materials by test preparation companies, and professional development about preparing students for the ACT. While not shown in the figure, math teachers were the most likely to receive any of the resource materials, by about eight additional percentage points. While teachers seem to be using materials from a variety of sources, in general, only a small proportion of teachers thought the materials they received were very helpful. It was most common for teachers to rate the materials they received as "somewhat helpful."

Practice exams were the most popular resource materials. Not only did almost all teachers receive them, but more than 90 percent of teachers who received practice exams said they were helpful, and more than 40 percent said they were very helpful. This is consistent with teacher and student interviews that suggested most test preparation occurring in classes consisted of going through practice exams. Most core subject teachers also reported receiving instructional guides by ACT and materials produced by test preparation companies, and almost all (91 percent) who received these materials felt they were helpful.

About 75 percent of core subject teachers said in the 2007 survey that they received professional development on preparing students for the ACT. None of the teachers we interviewed in 2005 mentioned professional development on the ACT, and this might reflect changes in practice over the last two years. In the survey, math teachers were more likely than other teachers to report receiving professional development around the ACT. It was least common for teachers to receive lesson plans around the ACT, but 63 percent did report receiving these lesson plans and more than 80 percent of those teachers felt they were helpful.

The content that teachers cover also varies considerably. Our interviews found that most teach such test-taking strategies as process of elimination, skimming, and skipping ahead. Others go through the different academic skills tested on the ACT, specific to their subject. Many teachers discuss academic skills as they go through practice tests.

There is also variability in the degree to which teachers cover the ACT versus the non-ACT portions of the PSAE. While few students care about their scores on the non-ACT portions of the test, many teachers spend class time on practice for those portions, particularly the Work Keys section (see Figure 9, page 23). However, the time teachers spend on the non-ACT portions of the test varies considerably.

FIGURE 18

Most teachers use a variety of test preparation materials; they find practice exams the most helpful

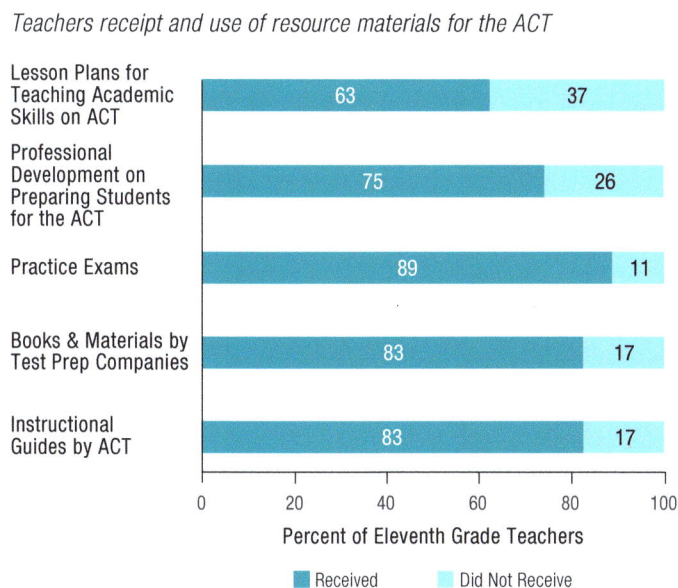

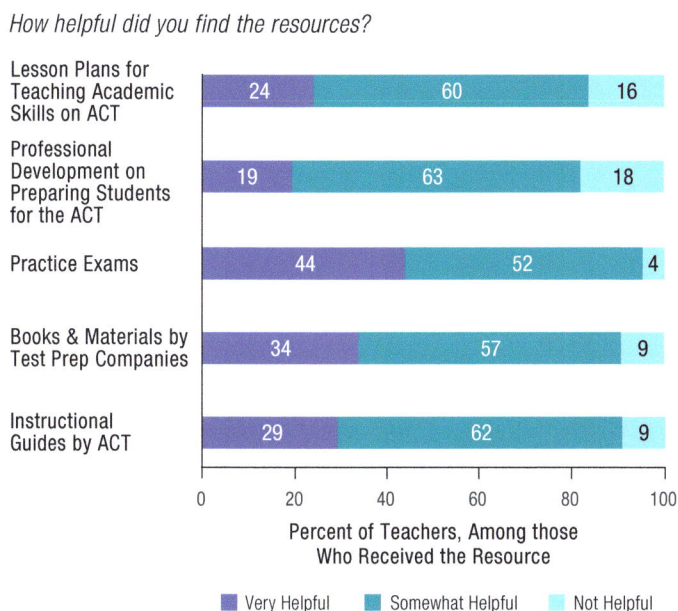

Teachers receipt and use of resource materials for the ACT

Resource	Received	Did Not Receive
Lesson Plans for Teaching Academic Skills on ACT	63	37
Professional Development on Preparing Students for the ACT	75	26
Practice Exams	89	11
Books & Materials by Test Prep Companies	83	17
Instructional Guides by ACT	83	17

Percent of Eleventh Grade Teachers

■ Received ■ Did Not Receive

How helpful did you find the resources?

Resource	Very Helpful	Somewhat Helpful	Not Helpful
Lesson Plans for Teaching Academic Skills on ACT	24	60	16
Professional Development on Preparing Students for the ACT	19	63	18
Practice Exams	44	52	4
Books & Materials by Test Prep Companies	34	57	9
Instructional Guides by ACT	29	62	9

Percent of Teachers, Among those Who Received the Resource

■ Very Helpful ■ Somewhat Helpful ■ Not Helpful

Note: These frequencies are based on 11th-grade teachers surveyed in spring 2007.

national averages are calculated based on 18 months of learning—from the fall tenth-grade administration of PLAN to the spring eleventh-grade administration of ACT. However, when students consider their likely improvement, they are thinking about the PLAN exam they take in the fall of eleventh grade compared to the ACT they take in the spring, a period of only six months.

Beyond misconceptions about the relationship of PLAN scores with ACT scores, there are general misconceptions about how practice test scores are related to real ACT scores. There is a general faith among students that scores continue to increase each time they take the test. Students tend to believe their actual score will be better than the score they received on the last practice exam. Furthermore, students believe they can always retake the test and get a better score.

> "They suggest that you take it two times. Supposedly your score gets higher the more times you take it, and [the colleges] take the highest score."—Student

However, scores do not necessarily improve with repeated attempts after a student has gained familiarity with the test.[45] On their website, ACT states that only 55 percent of students retaking the test received a higher score; the rest received the same score or a lower score.[46] Fifteen of the students we interviewed said they retook the ACT during their senior year. Among them, few had prepared for the retake, and only one student's score improved.

Thus, students are getting the message that doing well on the ACT is mostly about test practice. They are preparing for the ACT by spending large amounts of class time learning testing strategies and reviewing practice tests items. However, the ways in which many students are practicing provide a false sense about the content and pacing of the exam. Misconceptions about practice tests lead many students to have false perceptions about their likely scores. Students' descriptions of test preparation suggest that they see preparation for the ACT as an activity that is separate from the other work they are doing in their classes, and they see little value in it beyond preparation for the test:

Interviewer: So would you say that what you're
learning in your classes is important?
Student: I don't think I'm going to use none of that
in the future, what I'm learning now, but I guess it's
important for right now...because of the ACT test,...
but in the future.... I want to be a writer because I
like writing, but she just makes it boring to me.

Teachers' descriptions of test preparation are consistent with students' perceptions in that most describe test preparation as going through test items. However, from teachers we can see there is substantial variety in the types of materials that they use and in the content of the practice items they give students. Some teachers we interviewed felt they had devised good strategies for helping students prepare for the exam; however, many more were unsatisfied with the way that test preparation was delivered in their classes. In general, teachers' strategies seemed idiosyncratic—each was trying to figure out how best to do test preparation (see "The Tools Teachers Are Using to Prepare Students for the ACT," page 34).

Teachers Have Problems Integrating ACT Preparation into Course Instruction

"In the world of ACT prep, there's this conundrum of how do we make it relative to what we are doing?"—Teacher

"I think [teachers] might get frustrated and just take sample tests and go over the answers."—Teacher

Uniformly, teachers we interviewed felt conflicted about spending class time on preparation for the ACT. Each teacher talked about how preparing for the ACT interfered with course goals and took time away from instruction in the subject. They had struggled to figure out how to incorporate test preparation in a way that they thought was instructionally appropriate, and most had resigned themselves to spending less time on some of the topics they wanted to cover in their course. Respondents to the 2007 survey were not as uniformly negative as teachers in our interview sample about incorporating ACT preparation into

their courses, but many teachers are clearly struggling; more than half (56 to 67 percent) of teachers in each core subject agreed that test preparation interrupted their lesson flow, including a quarter of English teachers who agreed strongly (see Figure 19).

It may seem odd that so many teachers are struggling with ACT preparation, because the test is supposed to be aligned with high school courses and state standards. ACT, Inc., actively works to map the content of its tests onto the topics that high school teachers teach and to be consistent with educational standards from 49 states.[47] The company is explicit about this in its test description, which states that "scores on the tests have a direct relationship to the students' educational progress in curriculum-related areas."[48] They survey middle school, high school, and college teachers every three to five years in a national curriculum survey to determine the importance of skills and content knowledge students have, and then use this information to gauge the content of the EPAS. Furthermore, the ACT has been adopted for the major portion of the PSAE, because ACT, Inc., has demonstrated that the skills it tests are aligned with state standards.

Yet, ACT, Inc., affirms that the test is one of general achievement, not a measure of specific course content. In its materials, ACT, Inc., notes that it is not a test of high school course content, because "high school courses vary extensively," and "such tests might not measure students' skills in problem solving and in the integration of knowledge from a variety of courses."[49] Furthermore, where there are differences between high school teachers' and college instructors' reports of the skills students need, the ACT uses college instructors' reports to guide test content.[50] ACT, Inc.'s curriculum survey shows that college instructors and high school teachers tend to believe different skills and content are important.[51] Testing the skills students will need in college makes sense for a test designed to gauge readiness for college, but the test structure bears little resemblance to the type of test that would measure the learning goals of a typical eleventh-grade high school course.

FIGURE 19

Most teachers agree test preparation disrupts lessons

Test prep interrupts lesson flow

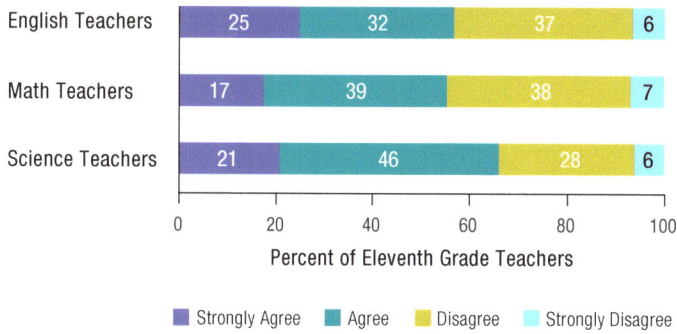

English Teachers	25	32	37	6
Math Teachers	17	39	38	7
Science Teachers	21	46	28	6

Percent of Eleventh Grade Teachers

■ Strongly Agree   ■ Agree   ■ Disagree   ■ Strongly Disagree

The Disconnect between High School Instruction and the ACT

The disconnect between high school instruction and the structure of the ACT exam is consistent with the disconnect identified between high school teachers' goals and the skills students need in college. Research has found that cognitive and metacognitive abilities—skills in analysis, interpretation, precision and accuracy, problem solving and reasoning—are considered much more important by college instructors than content knowledge in specific courses.[52] Correspondingly, the ACT does not test specific content knowledge, but instead requires students to "*apply* the content knowledge and reasoning skills they've acquired in their course work to *high-level* tasks . . . often requiring the integration of proficiencies and skills from various high school courses."[53] Yet, high school teachers consistently emphasize broad content knowledge as more important than developing the analytic skill sets known to be important for college.[54] The differences in skill and content emphasis between traditional high school courses and college present a challenge for teachers of specific eleventh-grade courses who are expected to prepare their students for a general skills-based test of college readiness. The ACT structure does not match the traditional high school curriculum structure in a number of ways, as described below.

Much of the content of any one course is not tested on the ACT. With the possible exception of math courses, much of the content in any given course will not be tested on the ACT. While teachers are likely to want their students to gain the skills tested on the ACT in their subject areas, these skills are often not primary goals. Consider eleventh-grade English, which might be seen as the classes that are most strongly tested by the ACT since two of the four subject tests are reading and English. In our interviews, we asked teachers what their goals were for their classes. Since eleventh-grade English covers British literature, students read Shakespeare's plays and the romantic poets. Teachers said their goals were to cover particular readings and literary periods and styles.[55] Yet, knowledge of British literature is not tested on the ACT. Whether students can identify various literary eras, the authors related to them, and their works is superfluous to what is tested on the ACT, but very important to teachers who want to cover British literature. While the ACT is used for accountability purposes, the skills it tests are not those of highest priority to high school classroom teachers. It is not surprising that the majority of eleventh-grade English and science teachers do not believe that the ACT is a good measure of student learning in high school (see Figure 17, page 31). This issue is less problematic in math, and math teachers were most likely to agree that the ACT is a good measure of what students have learned in high school.

Only a portion of the questions in any subject test measure skills from a particular class. While the content that math teachers emphasize is likely to be included on the ACT, math teachers face a different problem in that only a small portion of the exam will test skills that they would normally cover in their eleventh-grade course. Instead, the test requires integrating skills learned across subjects over many years. Consider the content of the ACT math exam, shown in Appendix C. A typical eleventh-grade class is Algebra II, and 15 percent of the ACT math exam content is devoted to intermediate algebra and another 7 percent to trigonometry, which is likely to be covered with advanced algebra. But almost a quarter of the test covers plane geometry, another 15 percent covers coordinate geometry, and another quarter covers pre-algebra topics. The ACT teacher guide lists topics that would be covered in a variety of different math classes. As teachers think about how to prepare their students for the ACT, they often feel they need to cover not just the content in their particular course, but the content in all of the math courses that students have taken in high school. If an Algebra II teacher only covers topics from Algebra II, she will only cover about a quarter of the topics on the math subject test—yet she may feel responsible for preparing students for the entire subject test. While this issue is most obvious in math, the problem also arises in other subjects; the science test takes questions from different science courses (biology, chemistry, earth/space science, and physics), and the English section tests skills that students were likely to have learned in earlier grades and elementary school (e.g., sentence structure).

> "With that test they go with things way back. You know it's not from this year but things that you've learned since freshman year. Or sophomore year. I kind of did really bad sophomore year. So the stuff from sophomore year I didn't know."—Student

Skills are often tested indirectly and presented in a different style than typical. Finally, the way in which the ACT tests subject-specific skills may be very different from how teachers test those skills in their classes. In math, for example, students need particular content knowledge, such as the properties of triangles and solving quadratic equations. But only a small subset of the ACT math questions are straightforward, one-step problems that clearly test one specific skill. Often the skills that students need to answer a particular math question are not immediately obvious, and there may be different ways to solve the same problem. Consider problem 10 in the sample math items in Appendix A. This item could be solved by using simultaneous equations. But instead of simply presenting simultaneous equations, the problem requires students to figure out that they can use simultaneous equations, write and solve the equations, and then take the solutions they obtained by solving the equations and multiply them together to come up with the correct answer. This is typical of most of the ACT problems—first students need to figure out a way to solve the problem, drawing on many potential skills they have learned across classes. Then they need to solve the problem, using

those skills in a multistep method and then using the solution to answer the problem in the specific way that it has been posed. Compare this to the way students often tackle math problems in their classes—where the skill being tested is defined by the unit they are working on in class and the application of the skill produces the answer without any further steps.

There are parallel issues in English. The English portion of the ACT tests grammar and writing—skills that are taught in English classes. In high school English classes, grammar often is taught by identifying parts of speech and diagramming sentences—and these are the skills that the eleventh-grade teachers we interviewed said they were teaching to prepare students for the ACT. However, the ACT never asks students to identify parts of speech or diagram sentences. Instead, it asks students to make decisions about the best way to edit text (see Appendix A, page 64). Certainly, students can draw on their knowledge of parts of speech to answer the questions, but that skill is one step removed from what is actually tested. Furthermore, many of the editing decisions will demand they consider the context of a sentence within the entire passage—requiring students to go beyond proper grammatical usage to think about the best way to write a sentence given the meaning the author wants to convey.

The reading test more closely matches some of the teachers' goals about understanding text and literary styles, but students' course assignments are likely to contain questions on characters, quotes, and plot that can be directly derived from a text. In contrast, ACT reading questions ask students to make inferences not directly stated in the text. Moreover, ACT reading passages are largely nonfiction, whereas nonfiction reading may be rare in some high schools.

The science portion of the exam is more clearly tied to specific subjects, but it does not test specific content knowledge in those classes—students do not have to rely on memorization of facts or apply scientific principles. Instead, the science portion asks students to interpret data and evaluate hypotheses. This may be very different from the manner in which some science teachers test their subject.[56] The reading portion of the test is applicable to science and social science classes, containing passages that require students to interpret scientific and social scientific text—but the questions do not simply ask students to identify information in the reading passage as they might do in a typical class (e.g., read a text to learn about definitions, processes, historical dates, etc.). Instead, the questions require students to consider different interpretations of the text and construct meaning from the text in ways that are not explicitly stated as facts.

Thus, the structure of the ACT presents significant test preparation challenges for teachers working under a traditional organization of courses, especially if they are using conventional methods for teaching their subjects. Many teachers are struggling with how to incorporate ACT preparation into their classes without taking time away from the topics and skills they believe are important to cover in their classes. Uncertainty about how to integrate ACT preparation into regular course work leads teachers to simply go through practice items as their main strategy for test preparation. In doing so, they resign themselves to spending less time on their subject and interrupting their course flow.

Content-based strategies are often misaligned with the test. Many teachers try to incorporate substantive subject matter learning into test preparation—covering the topics in their subject area that will be tested. However, it can be challenging to cover a broad array of topics they would not otherwise teach. In interviews, some teachers said they developed their own units to help students learn the content to be tested, often trying to cover a year of material in a matter of weeks.

> "So we crashed the geometry that you need to know for the ACT [went through it quickly], you'll probably never see it again in your life."—Eleventh-grade math teacher

Others introduced material from lower-level classes throughout the year. These are logical approaches. Yet, the result is broad and shallow instruction, with little time to do deep problem-solving work within any given topic. In the end, even substantive test preparation often ends up looking a lot like practice tests—lots of practice questions, nothing in depth, and moving from discrete topic to discrete topic.

Some teachers think the ACT is a test of basic skills or a curriculum-based test, and these perceptions can lead teachers to change their practice in counterproductive ways. The perception that it is a basic skills test may arise from the multiple-choice format or the common use of the PLAN as a practice test. Perceptions that it is a curriculum-based test might come from the ACT teacher guides, which list the many topics and skills that might be included on the tests, or from knowledge of the state learning standards that the PSAE is supposed to test. As a result of these misperceptions, one math teacher said she switched from inquiry-based to topic-based approaches, because she felt pressure to cover all of the content areas covered on the ACT. Yet, the math test is more consistent with inquiry-based instruction than topic-based instruction. An English teacher complained she had to give up a unit in which students write and edit a research paper to improve their writing skills so they would have time for test preparation, yet the ACT specifically tests students' editing skills. Thus, lack of understanding of the test and misalignment with typical eleventh-grade curricula, can lead teachers to engage in practices that they themselves recognize are not good.

Students Are Not Benefiting from All the Time Spent on Test Preparation

Practice tests have become instructional tools in large numbers of eleventh-grade classrooms. Is this a good tool for producing learning gains and improvements in ACT scores? From what we know about learning, this is unlikely. The ACT is designed as an assessment tool, not an instructional tool. The items are not organized in a meaningful way, and the information is presented absent of context. Research on learning shows that to develop competence, students need to understand facts in the context of a conceptual framework; this helps them organize information in ways that facilitate their retrieval and application to new problems.[57] Simply going through random test items will make it difficult for students to develop conceptual frameworks, retain and retrieve information they have learned, and build on their base of knowledge. Ironically, because the ACT is a problem-solving test, students need conceptual frameworks that will allow them to use information (facts, vocabulary) they have not seen before to figure out problems.

Students' descriptions of test preparation in their classes suggest that little learning is occurring. They describe test preparation as boring and disconnected from anything else they are learning in their class or need for the future. Yet, they are willing to sit through it because they believe it will improve their scores:

> "It's getting real irritating because every class we have to do ACT work. . . . Yeah it's important, I know it's important, but I'm just saying that it is irritating because we are doing the same thing basically over and over."—Eleventh-grade student

As discussed in the sidebar "Prior Research on the Effects of Test Preparation on ACT Scores" (see page 24), other researchers have found little to no positive effects of coaching, item practice, or learning testing strategies on ACT scores. Data from CPS corroborate those findings. To examine the effects of test preparation on ACT scores, we compared students' ACT scores to students' and teachers' reports of the ways in which they prepared for the ACT, both outside of class hours and during regular class time. Using statistical models, we took out differences in ACT scores that could be explained by other factors, including students' academic skills prior to eleventh grade (their PLAN score from the beginning of eleventh grade and their eighth-grade test scores); their course grades and absence rates in eleventh grade; the types of courses in which they were enrolled in eleventh grade (e.g., physics vs. earth science); their background and demographic characteristics (race, gender, economic status); characteristics of their classrooms (including teacher characteristics), such as the average ability level of students; and characteristics of their schools, such as the percentage of low-income students. (See Appendix D for details on the statistical models.) We used these models so that any differences we observed in ACT scores could not be attributed simply to differences in the types of schools or classes students attended or to students' background characteristics. Thus, we are comparing students, classrooms, and schools that would have had similar

pressure to show improvements in their scores (e.g., low-achieving schools to other similarly low-achieving schools). By controlling for students' PLAN scores in the fall of eleventh grade, differences in ACT scores represent changes attributable to the students' junior year (approximately six months of school). All eleventh-grade students, teachers, and schools that participated in the CCSR survey were included in these analyses.

Test Preparation Outside of Class Had Small and Inconsistent Relationships with Improvements in ACT Scores

Consistent with previous research, there was little evidence that ACT preparation classes taken outside of regular school hours helped students' scores. In 2007, CPS students who regularly attended an ACT preparation class outside of school hours had somewhat higher scores on the English subject test (by an average of 0.65 points), but only slightly higher scores on the math and science subject tests (by an average of 0.16 in math and 0.24 in science), and there was no significant difference in reading scores for students who took a preparation course compared to those who did not (see Figure 20). There were no differences in test scores between students who occasionally attended an ACT preparation class and those who never attended such a class.[58] These modest differences provide little support for the time and money spent on test preparation courses, except on the English subject test. Furthermore, they are overestimates of the actual effects of test preparation courses. Students who regularly attended an ACT preparation class are a select group who probably have particularly high stamina and motivation. They might also be the students who are working the hardest in their classes and earning good grades. Requiring students who would not ordinarily take an ACT preparation class to do so might not have as much of a positive effect on their ACT scores, because they wouldn't have these qualities.

To examine the effects of test preparation courses in a way that would be less likely to be biased by students' own characteristics, we also compared average ACT scores in schools where many students frequently attended an ACT preparation course to scores in schools where few students attended a preparation

FIGURE 20

Students who often attended an ACT prep class outside of regular school hours had slightly higher ACT scores than students who did not attend ACT prep class

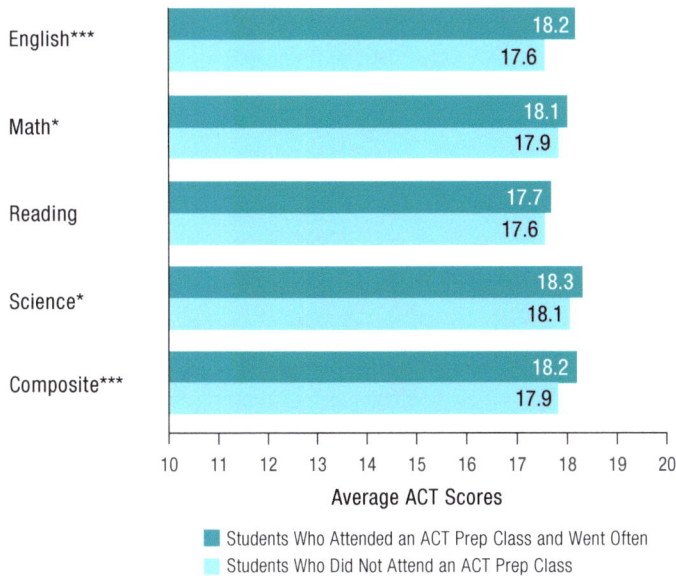

Subject	Students Who Attended an ACT Prep Class and Went Often	Students Who Did Not Attend an ACT Prep Class
English***	18.2	17.6
Math*	18.1	17.9
Reading	17.7	17.6
Science*	18.3	18.1
Composite***	18.2	17.9

Average ACT Scores

■ Students Who Attended an ACT Prep Class and Went Often
■ Students Who Did Not Attend an ACT Prep Class

Note: These averages are calculated from students who participated in the 2007 survey. These are the differences that remain after controlling for students' 11th grade PLAN scores, grades, and students' demographic, economic and achievement characteristics, course absences, teacher backgrounds, course enrollment, and school composition (see statistical models in Appendix D). Students who occasionally attended an ACT prep class did not show significantly different ACT scores than those who never attended an ACT prep class.
*p< .05   ***p< .001

FIGURE 21A

ACT scores were not higher in schools with many students taking the ACT prep classes

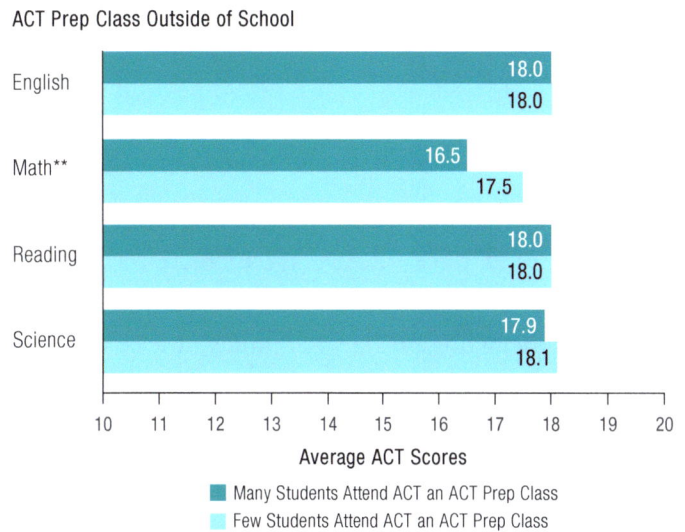

ACT Prep Class Outside of School

Subject	Many Students Attend an ACT Prep Class	Few Students Attend an ACT Prep Class
English	18.0	18.0
Math**	16.5	17.5
Reading	18.0	18.0
Science	17.9	18.1

Average ACT Scores

■ Many Students Attend ACT an ACT Prep Class
■ Few Students Attend ACT an ACT Prep Class

FIGURE 21B

ACT scores were slightly higher in schools where almost all students take full, timed practice tests

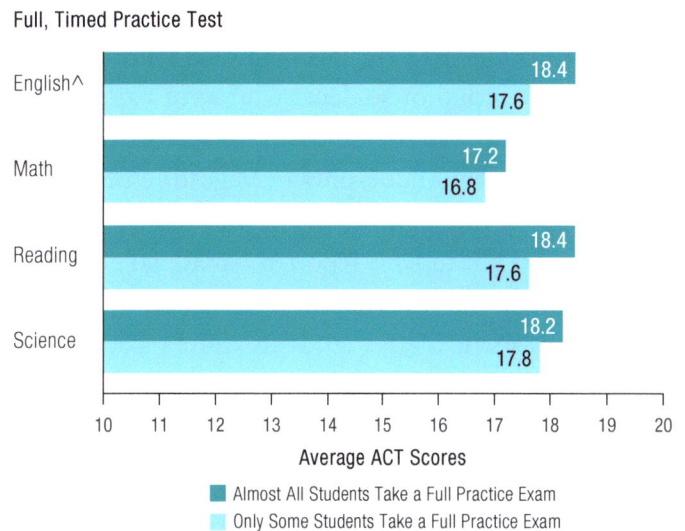

Full, Timed Practice Test

Subject	Almost All Students Take a Full Practice Exam	Only Some Students Take a Full Practice Exam
English^	18.4	17.6
Math	17.2	16.8
Reading	18.4	17.6
Science	18.2	17.8

Average ACT Scores

■ Almost All Students Take a Full Practice Exam
■ Only Some Students Take a Full Practice Exam

Note: These difference between "Many" and "Few" students attending an ACT prep class is 25 percentage points (e.g., 15% versus 40% of students; the difference between "Almost All" students taking a practice exam and "Some" students is 30 percentage points (e.g., 90% versus 60%). Each difference represents two standard deviations across schools. These figures control for students' PLAN scores, backgrounds, teacher and school characteristics, as described in Appendix D.
^p< .10   **p< .01

course. We know that some schools offered Saturday and after school test prep classes, and we expect that more students in these schools would attend such classes, regardless of their individual characteristics. These comparisons of schools do not show any advantage to offering test preparation classes to students. ACT scores were not higher, on average, in schools where many students frequently attended an ACT preparation class outside of regular school hours, compared to schools where few students attended such an ACT class, controlling for students' background characteristics and school characteristics (see Figure 21a).[59] In fact, average math scores were significantly lower the more that a school's eleventh-graders reported attending such a class.[60] This suggests no benefit to such courses—the benefits seen among students likely occur because students who take a preparation class outside of school are a select group of students within their schools. There could be some selection issues at the school level, in that schools that have not been successful with classroom instruction may be more likely to try to improve scores

by offering preparation classes outside of school, or students who feel they are not learning sufficiently in their classes might be more likely to pursue assistance outside of class. Thus, these school comparisons may underestimate the benefits of test preparation classes. On the other hand, these findings are consistent with those of other researchers who have also found small to negative effects of test preparation classes on ACT scores. Testing strategies may be ineffectual, or they may distract students from simply engaging intellectually in the exam.

Gaining Familiarity with the Test through Full, Timed Practice Is Beneficial, But There Are Limits to the Benefits of Retaking the Test

Other researchers have found that among students who retake the ACT once, the average increase in scores is just 0.7, and subsequent retakes show smaller gains.[61] In CPS, students who said they had taken at least one full timed practice test since January showed higher ACT scores than students who did not take a full timed practice test (see Figure 22). These differences were modest, ranging from a low of 0.15 on the math subject test to a high of 0.33 on the science subject test. There were smaller benefits associated with taking more than one timed practice test; the differences in scores for students who took two or more tests, compared to those who took one test, were fewer than 0.10 points for each subject test. It is possible that students who took repeated tests were a select group of students who were particularly motivated to do well on the exam. When we compare average scores by school, only average English scores came close to being significantly higher in those schools where almost all students reported having taken a full, timed practice test since January, compared to schools where only about half of students did so (see Figure 21b). However, we do not know the extent to which students already had taken full, timed tests prior to January, and so were already familiar with the test. Given that there are generally positive relationships between practice tests and ACT scores, these results suggest modest benefits for students' ACT scores from familiarity with testing conditions, but there are limits to what can be achieved by test familiarity.

Test Practice during Students' Regular Classes Does Not Boost ACT Scores

We asked students and teachers many questions about how they were preparing for the PSAE during class time. Each of these questions showed either no relationship or a negative relationship with improvements from PLAN to ACT.

FIGURE 22

ACT scores were slightly higher among students who took a full, timed practice test compared to those who did not. However, there were diminishing benefits to multiple practice tests

Number of full, timed practice tests students took since January:

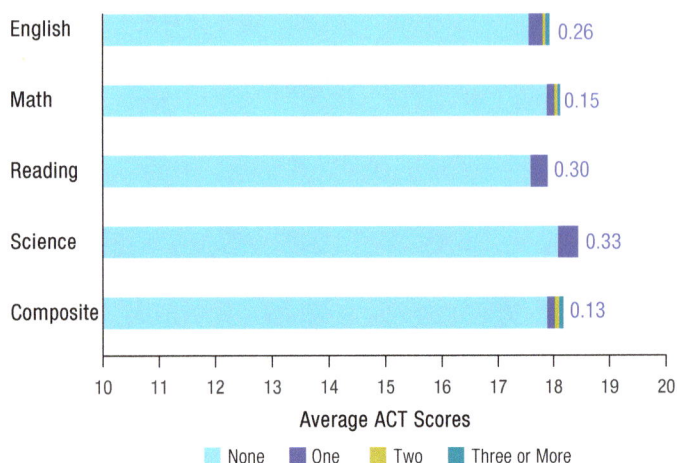

Note: The numbers in this chart are the difference in scores between students taking one practice test and zero tests; all are significant at p< .05. Only the composite score shows a significant difference for students taking multiple tests compared to those taking just one full, timed practice test. These averages are calculated from students who participated in the 2007 survey and control for students' 11th grade PLAN scores, grades, and students' demographic, economic and achievement characteristics, course absences, teacher backgrounds, course enrichment, and school composition (see statistical models in Appendix D).

FIGURE 23

ACT scores were slightly lower in schools where teachers spent large amounts of class time on test preparation

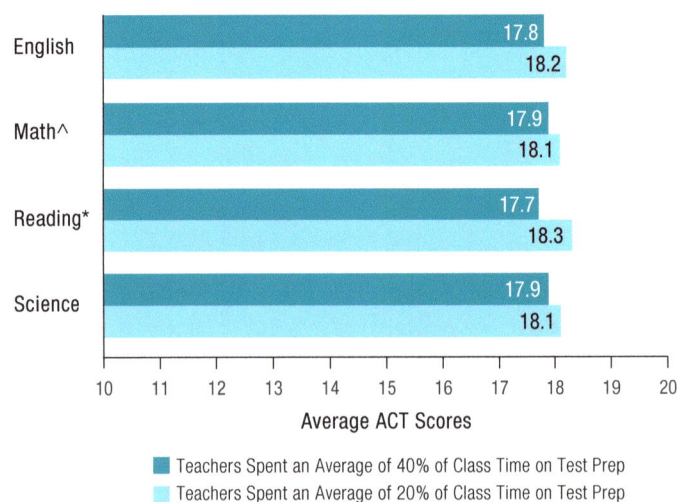

Note: These differences control for students' PLAN scores, backgrounds, teacher and school characteristics, as described in the Appendix D, using data from Spring 2007. Teachers were asked what percentage of class time, since January, had been spent on practice tests and test-taking strategies. Responses were aggregated to the school level using a Tobit model, which adjusted for responses that were outside of the potential response categories (i.e., greater than 50%, the highest response category).
^p< .10 *p< .05

In the 2007 survey, we asked teachers what percentage of class time they had spent having students take practice tests and learn test-taking strategies. Figure 23 shows average test scores for schools in which core subject eleventh-grade teachers spent an average of 40 percent of their time on test preparation in the spring term, compared to schools in which teachers spent 20 percent of their time on test preparation. In no subject were ACT scores higher in schools that used substantial class time for test preparation, and reading scores were more than half a point lower. We also asked teachers how often they engaged in different types of test preparation activities, including practicing Work Keys,

learning test-taking strategies, going through practice tests, and taking timed tests. Regardless of the type of test preparation activity, schools where many eleventh-grade teachers did ACT preparation intensively in the spring term did not show higher ACT scores than other schools (see Figure 24). In fact, schools where many teachers frequently taught test-taking strategies (once a week or more) showed lower scores on the reading and English subject tests than schools where few teachers emphasized test-taking strategies, by about a half-point. Intensive Work Keys practice also was associated with lower scores on the reading subject test. Schools where most teachers reported using ACT resource materi-

FIGURE 24

Regardless of the type of test preparation emphasized, schools where most teachers do intensive ACT preparation showed the same or lower ACT scores as schools where few teachers do intensive ACT preparation

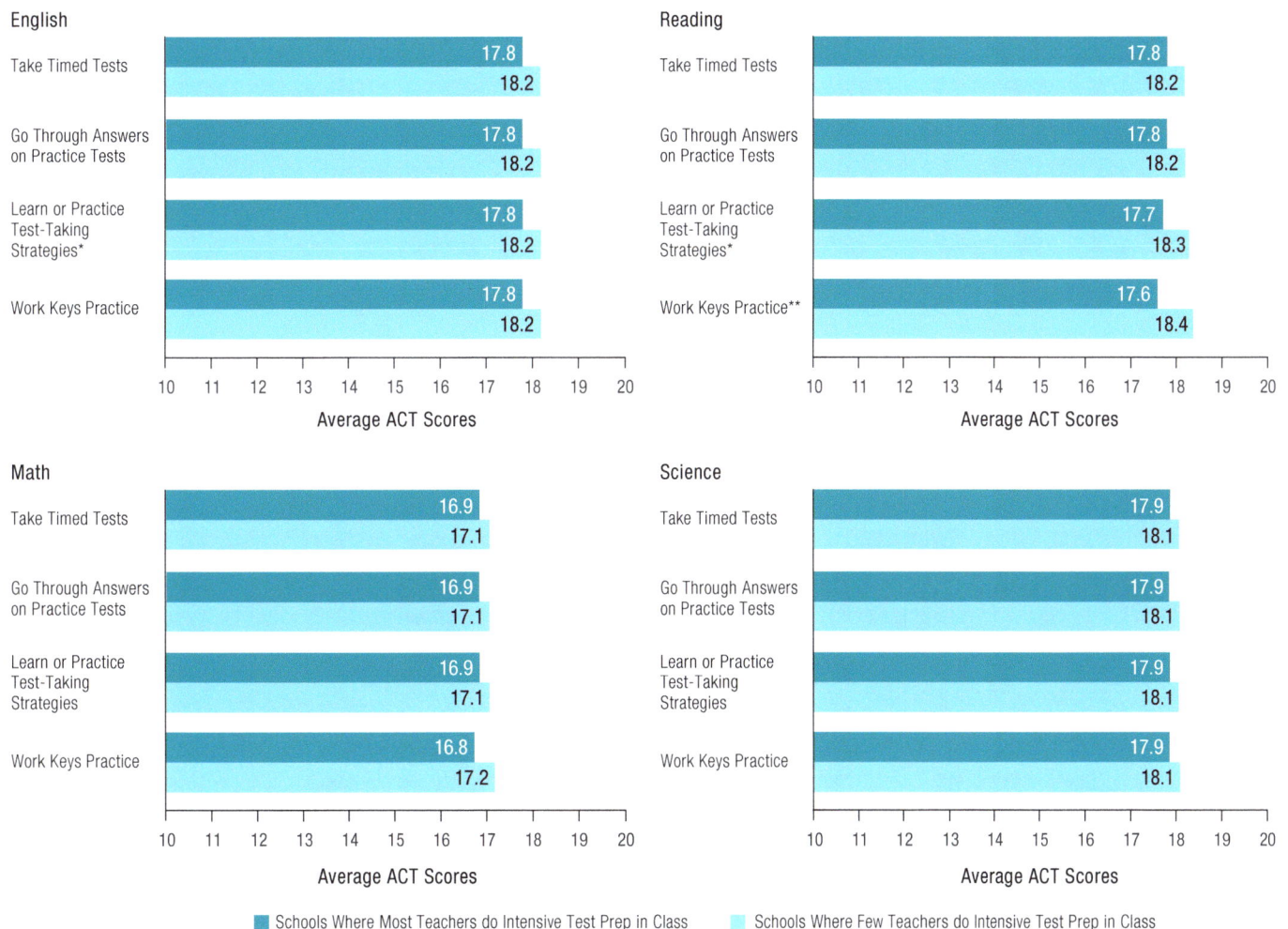

Schools Where Most Teachers do Intensive Test Prep in Class

Schools Where Few Teachers do Intensive Test Prep in Class

Note: Intensive preparation refers to doing the test preparation activity once a week or more in the spring term. The difference between schools where "Most Teachers" versus "Few Teachers" do intensive prep is 50 percentage points (e.g., 60% compared to 10% of teachers), which is about two standard deviations across schools. The difference was calculated through statistical models measuring the change in average scores for every percentage point increase in the number of teachers doing intensive preparation. These differences control for students' PLAN score, backgrounds, teacher and school characteristics, as described in the Appendix D.
*p< .05 **p< .01

als also showed substantially lower ACT scores than schools where few teachers used ACT resource materials (see Figure 25). Schoolwide use of materials by test preparation companies and ACT instructional guides, in particular, showed negative relationships with ACT scores on all subject tests by more than a half-point.

Students' reports of the particular ways that they prepared for the exam did not seem to matter for their math or reading scores. We asked students the extent to which they did activities such as taking practice tests, learning testing strategies, and studying particular skills as they prepared for specific subject tests (students' responses to these questions are shown in Figure 15, page 30). None of the questions showed a consistent significant relationship with either math or reading scores.[62] In contrast, English subject test scores showed a positive relationship with taking practice tests and going over test answers—students who reported doing these activities a "great deal" when preparing for the exam had scores that were about 0.4 points

FIGURE 25

Average ACT scores were lower the more that teachers reported using ACT materials by test-prep companies and ACT instructional guides

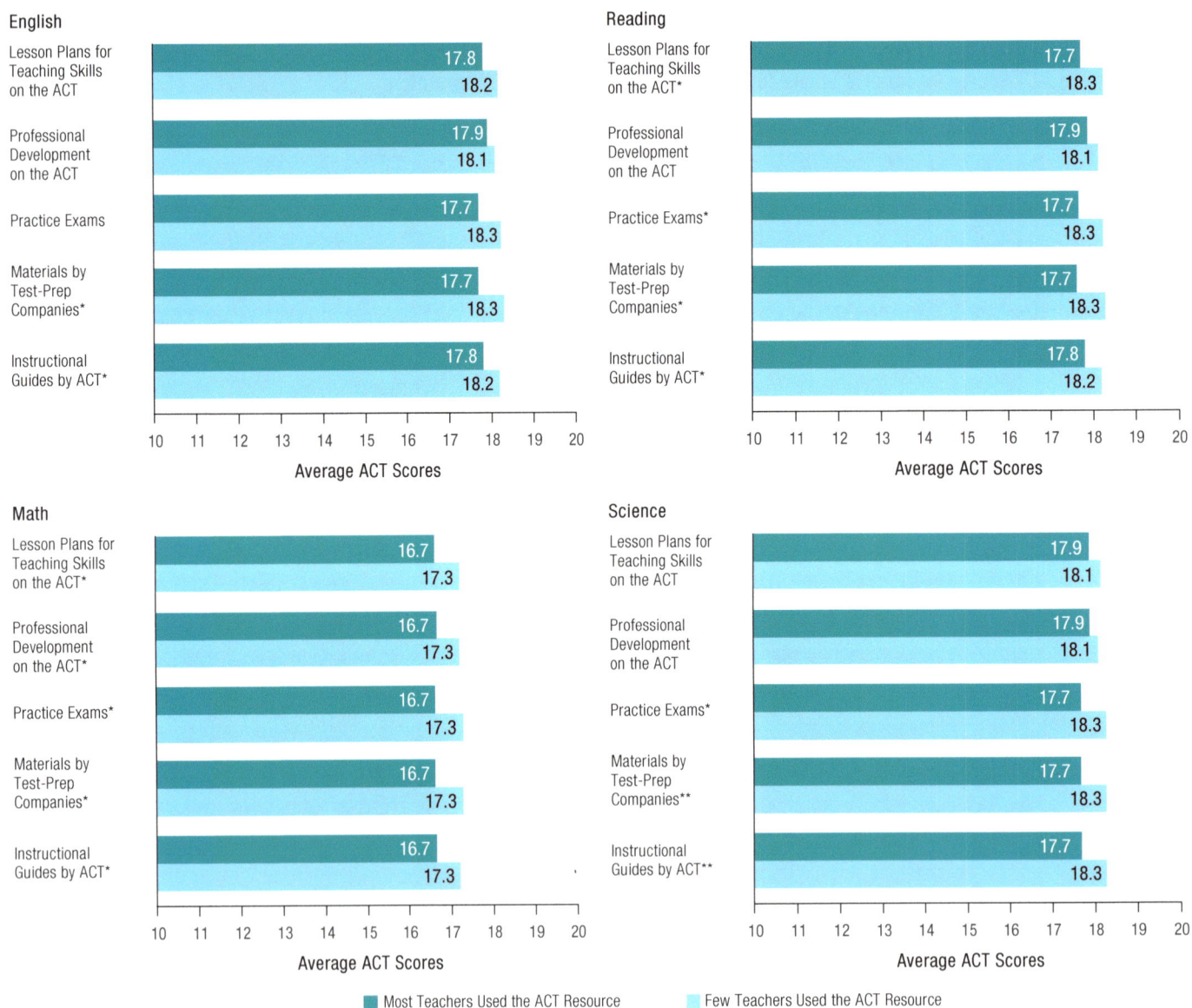

English

	Most Teachers Used the ACT Resource	Few Teachers Used the ACT Resource
Lesson Plans for Teaching Skills on the ACT	17.8	18.2
Professional Development on the ACT	17.9	18.1
Practice Exams	17.7	18.3
Materials by Test-Prep Companies*	17.7	18.3
Instructional Guides by ACT*	17.8	18.2

Average ACT Scores

Reading

	Most Teachers Used the ACT Resource	Few Teachers Used the ACT Resource
Lesson Plans for Teaching Skills on the ACT*	17.7	18.3
Professional Development on the ACT	17.9	18.1
Practice Exams*	17.7	18.3
Materials by Test-Prep Companies*	17.7	18.3
Instructional Guides by ACT*	17.8	18.2

Average ACT Scores

Math

	Most Teachers Used the ACT Resource	Few Teachers Used the ACT Resource
Lesson Plans for Teaching Skills on the ACT*	16.7	17.3
Professional Development on the ACT*	16.7	17.3
Practice Exams*	16.7	17.3
Materials by Test-Prep Companies*	16.7	17.3
Instructional Guides by ACT*	16.7	17.3

Average ACT Scores

Science

	Most Teachers Used the ACT Resource	Few Teachers Used the ACT Resource
Lesson Plans for Teaching Skills on the ACT	17.9	18.1
Professional Development on the ACT	17.9	18.1
Practice Exams*	17.7	18.3
Materials by Test-Prep Companies**	17.7	18.3
Instructional Guides by ACT**	17.7	18.3

Average ACT Scores

■ Most Teachers Used the ACT Resource   ■ Few Teachers Used the ACT Resource

Note: The difference in use represents a 60 percentage point difference across schools (e.g., 80% compared to 20% of teachers), which is about 2 standard deviations. These differences control for students' PLAN score, backgrounds, teacher and school characteristics, as described in the Appendix D.
*p< .05 **p< .01

higher on the English subject test than students who did not do these activities at all when preparing for the English portions of the exam. In addition, students who reported learning grammar rules a "great deal" when preparing for the English portion had English scores that were about 0.3 points higher than students in schools where preparation did not include grammar rules. There were no significant differences in English scores among students who reported doing practice tests, practice answers, and grammar "a little" or "some" when preparing for the test, compared to students who never did these activities. Thus, the English exam was the only subject test where increasing student familiarity by practicing the test seemed to improve scores, perhaps because the English portion of the exam is so different from the types of work students are most likely to encounter in their regular course work. However, this does not mean that substantial class time should be spent practicing for the English subject test. The questions to students did not gauge the amount of time students spent preparing, just what was emphasized when they did test preparation. These differences might also be biased by student selection factors, as the most hardworking students may be most likely to report doing activities "a lot." As discussed earlier, more class time on preparation was generally associated with smaller improvements on the English subject test, as well as the other subject tests.

Motivation Does Not Seem to Be a Key Factor behind Test Score Improvements

Besides engaging in test practice, many schools are emphasizing motivation for the PSAE/ACT as a key way to boost scores. To gauge the degree to which motivation and school emphasis on the test affect scores, we asked eleventh-grade students a series of questions about their motivation for the test and the degree to which their school emphasized doing well on the test (see "Student Survey Questions about Motivation and School Emphasis on the ACT"). We then compared their responses to their ACT scores using the statistical models that controlled for earlier tests, background characteristics, and school characteristics. None of the questions about motivation showed a consistent positive relationship with ACT scores. Students' own feelings

about the ACT and their perceptions of the degree to which their school was emphasizing the ACT did not seem to be key factors affecting their scores. This could be because the vast majority of students are motivated to do well on the test, so there is little more to be gained from increased pressure.

Student Survey Questions about Motivation and School Emphasis on the ACT

Survey questions about students' motivation for the ACT

How much do you agree with the following statements about the ACT/PSAE?

- It's important for me to do well on the ACT.
- ACT preparation in class is important for my future.
- We spend too much time in class preparing for the ACT.

Survey questions about students' perceptions of ACT preparation at their school

How much do you agree with the following statements about the ACT/PSAE?

- People at this school take the ACT seriously.
- My teachers have helped me prepare for the ACT.

During the month before the ACT how often did you prepare for the ACT in your regular classes?

Thus, it seems that much of what schools, teachers, and students are doing in preparation for the ACT is unrelated to high scores on the ACT. Teachers are struggling with how to incorporate ACT preparation into their classes, so they spend substantial amounts of time on motivation, strategies, practice test items, and cramming content coverage. However, there is little evidence that practice or test coaching helps—in fact, it seems to hurt students' scores. The sample items and content practice that teachers use in their classes are often not representative of the ACT items. The slow pace of test practice in classrooms does not give students a sense of timing for the test. And the broad content coverage that some teachers attempt is not representative of the deep problem-solving skills tested on the ACT. Most importantly, test preparation in classes is taking time away from in-depth subject matter instruction, and it is this work that seems to be most strongly tied to test scores, as discussed in the following chapter.

Correct

Approx ACT
SCORE

# Correct	Approx ACT Score
18	18
19-20	19
21-22	20
22-24	21
24-25	22
26	23
27	24
28	25
29	26
30	27

PRACTICE
135 - 1

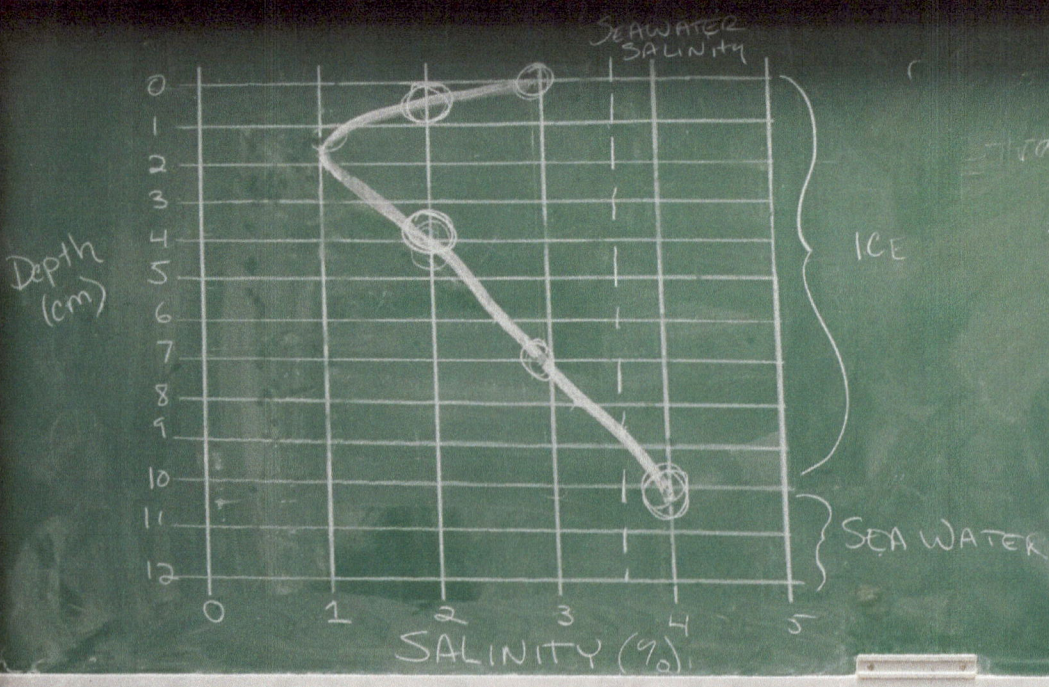

SEAWATER
SALINITY

Depth
(cm)

ICE

SEA WATER

SALINITY (‰)

A

C

Chapter 3

What Matters for Improvements on EPAS Tests?

If time spent on ACT preparation and emphasis on the ACT in schools does not benefit students' scores, what does matter? We can get some indication of what mattered by looking at the variables that were used to control for student, teacher, and classroom characteristics in measuring ACT scores. In addition, the CCSR surveys in 2007 included a number of questions about the kinds of work that students were doing in their classes. We can identify classroom practices related to test scores in the same way that we looked for relationships between test preparation and ACT scores—controlling for students' PLAN scores at the beginning of eleventh grade, course grades, and demographic, teacher, classroom, and school characteristics. These analyses suggest that what mattered for test scores were the quality of work students did in their academic classes and the academic climate of the school.

The strongest predictor of higher ACT scores in the spring was the grade that students' received in their classes. Among both low- and high-achieving students, those who did higher quality work in their classes as measured by their eleventh-grade course grades made much larger improvements than students with lower course grades that year. Figure 26 shows ACT scores by students' eleventh-grade grades, for students who had a PLAN score of 14, 17, or 19 in the fall. The subject-specific scores are graphed according to students' grades in corresponding eleventh-grade subjects. Regardless of whether students were initially high- or low-achieving, ACT scores were higher among students with higher course grades in the subject being tested. Students with As and Bs in eleventh grade had significantly higher scores than students with the same PLAN score who received Ds and Fs in their classes.

Students' course grades are a reflection of the quality of work that they have done in their classes. Therefore, it is not surprising that ACT scores were substantially higher the more that students and teachers reported appropriate academic behaviors among students, even when we statistically remove differences that can be explained by the types of students served by the school. (See Appendix E for details on how we measured academic behaviors.) As shown in Figure 27, the more that students reported that other students in their math and English classes help each other learn, treat each other with respect and get along together, the higher their

FIGURE 26

Students with higher grades in their eleventh grade courses made larger improvements from PLAN to ACT

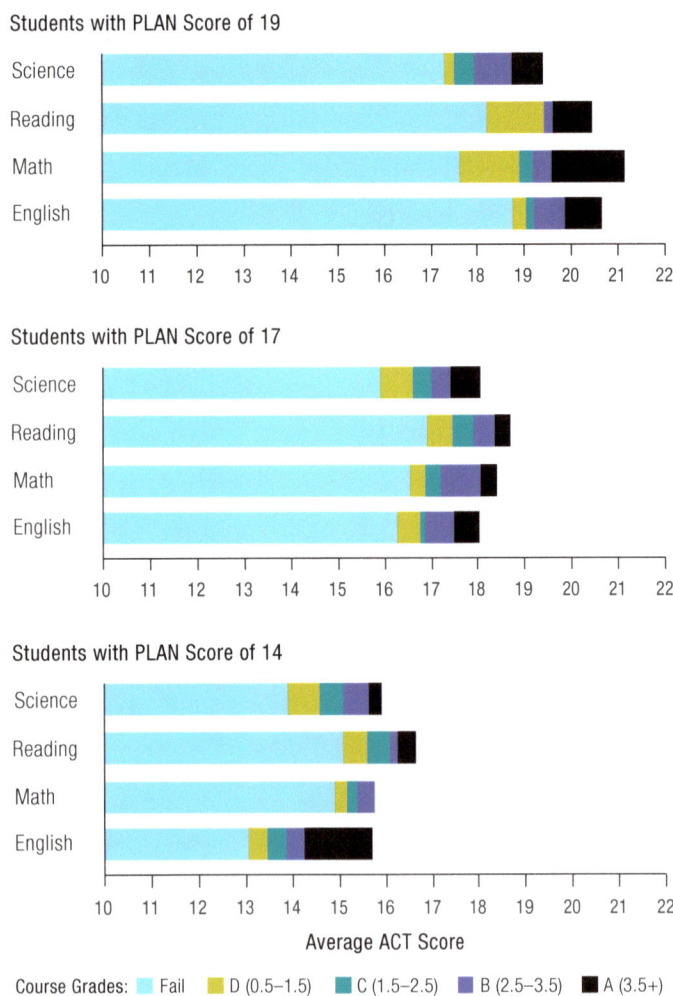

Students with PLAN Score of 19

Students with PLAN Score of 17

Students with PLAN Score of 14

Average ACT Score

Course Grades: ■ Fail ■ D (0.5–1.5) ■ C (1.5–2.5) ■ B (2.5–3.5) ■ A (3.5+)

Note: These show the average ACT score in the fall of 11th grade by course grade in subject tested, adjusted for student, teacher, and school characteristics as described in Appendix D, and including 11th grade PLAN score.

ACT scores, controlling for prior achievement—by 0.4 in science to 0.8 points in reading, on average. Likewise, schools in which eleventh-grade teachers reported better participation in their classes—more students coming to class on time, attending regularly, being prepared, paying attention, participating, and turning in homework—have substantially higher improvements in test scores than schools whose eleventh-grade teachers report poor academic behavior in their classes. Reading and science subject test scores are more than a half point higher in schools with high levels of positive student behavior, compared to poor student behavior, and English subject test scores are almost a point higher. These comparisons control for differences in the types of students schools serve, so it is not just that schools with better-prepared students show higher scores. As shown in Figure 28, good student academic behaviors are not found just in the top schools—even schools serving the most disadvantaged students vary considerably in their students' academic behaviors. Schools that are successful at getting students to participate appropriately in their regular course work are the schools that show the largest improvements in test scores during eleventh grade, from the fall PLAN to the spring ACT. Getting better ACT scores requires engaging instruction that brings out high-quality work from students.

Further evidence that the quality of regular classroom instruction matters is that test scores are higher among students whose teachers majored in the subject that they teach. Presumably, these are teachers who know their subject well and are better able to develop appropriate pedagogical strategies for their subject area. Students whose teachers had undergraduate majors in English have ACT English scores that are 0.67 points higher and reading scores that are 0.40 points higher than students whose teachers did not have an English major, controlling for students' backgrounds. Likewise, students whose teachers had undergraduate majors in math had ACT math scores 0.47 points higher than the students who did not have a teacher with a math major. However, these college degree effects disappear when we control for other teacher characteristics and the average ability levels of students' peers in their classrooms. Because teachers with degrees in the subject they teach are more likely to teach high-ability students, it

FIGURE 27

ACT scores are highest in schools with better student academic behavior in their classes, comparing schools that serve similar students

Students' Reports of Peers' Behavior in Their Class

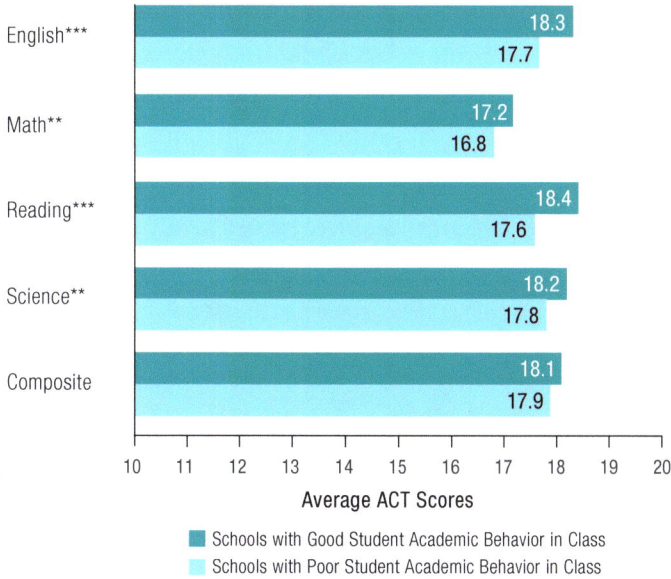

English***	18.3 / 17.7
Math**	17.2 / 16.8
Reading***	18.4 / 17.6
Science**	18.2 / 17.8
Composite	18.1 / 17.9

Average ACT Scores

■ Schools with Good Student Academic Behavior in Class
■ Schools with Poor Student Academic Behavior in Class

Teachers' Reports of Students' Behavior in Their Class

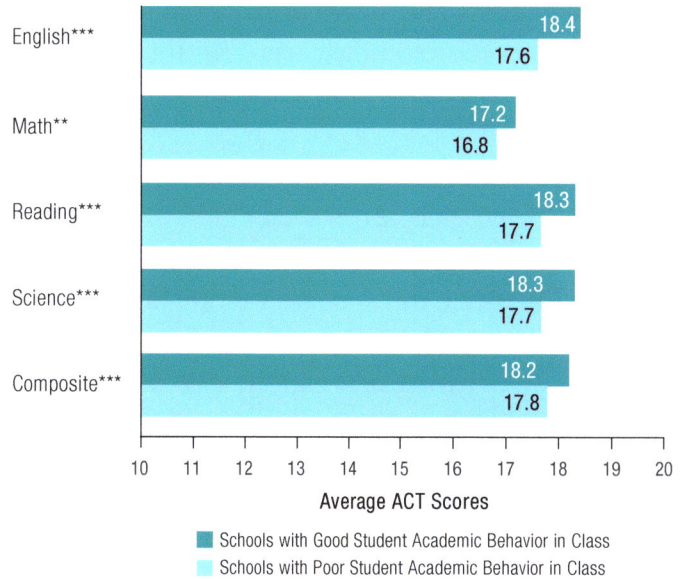

English***	18.4 / 17.6
Math**	17.2 / 16.8
Reading***	18.3 / 17.7
Science***	18.3 / 17.7
Composite***	18.2 / 17.8

Average ACT Scores

■ Schools with Good Student Academic Behavior in Class
■ Schools with Poor Student Academic Behavior in Class

Note: These differences control for students' 11th grade PLAN scores, backgrounds, teacher and school characteristics, as described in Appendix D. Teachers reported on: how many students come to class on time, attend class regularly, come prepared with appropriate supplies and books, regularly pay attention in class, actively participate in class activities, and always turn in their homework. Students reported on the extent to which students in their school: don't really care about each other, like to put others down, help each other learn, don't get along together very well, just look out for themselves, and treat each other with respect. **p< .01 ***p< .001

FIGURE 28

Students' reports of school climate vary considerably, even among schools serving similar types of students

Student Perceptions of Peer Behaviors

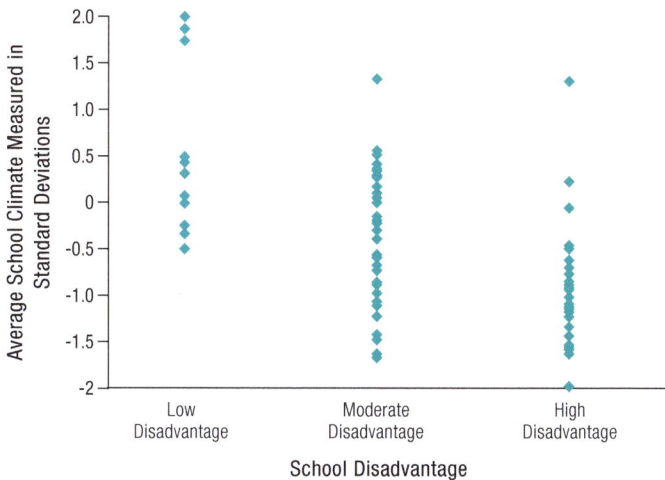

Student Reports of Schoolwide Future Orientation

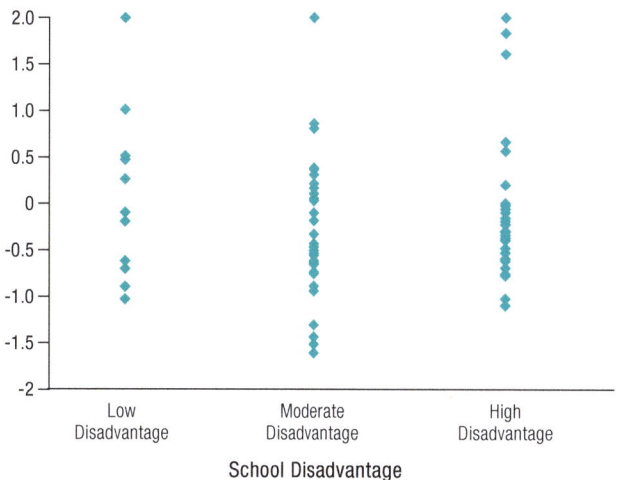

Note: Each symbol represents one high school. Disadvantage is measured as a combination of percent low-income students in the school, average incoming 9th grade EXPLORE scores, and poverty levels in students' residential neighborhoods. High disadvantage schools enroll 85-100% low-income students and their average EXPLORE score ranges from 11.8-13.7. Climate measures are represented in standard deviation units and trimmed at two standard deviations above and below the mean.

is difficult to separate out the effects of teacher background from peer effects. However, these relationships are suggestive that students learn more when they have teachers with more subject area knowledge.

In addition, the kind of day-to-day work students do in their classes relates to their scores on the ACT. We asked students the extent to which they do instructional tasks considered good practice in their English, math, and science classes. A number of practices in English, math, and science classes showed significant, positive relationships with ACT scores in all subject tests (see Table 5). In general, these practices are aligned with the skills tested on the ACT. For example, English subject test scores were particularly high in classrooms where students regularly improve a piece of writing as a class or in partners—a skill that is directly tested on the ACT. In addition, students who reported writing five or more papers, across all of their classes, in which they defended their point of view or their ideas had significantly higher English scores than other students with similar backgrounds. Science subject test scores were particularly high in classrooms where students regularly used evidence to support an argument or hypothesis and found information from graphs and tables—skills directly tested on the ACT. Reading subject test scores were particularly high in classrooms where students regularly debated the meaning of a reading, and math subject test scores were particularly high in classrooms where students discussed solutions to problems with other students.

Schools with particularly high "schoolwide future orientation" showed higher ACT scores, controlling for prior achievement, compared to other schools serving similar students, as shown in Figure 29. These were schools where students and teachers felt that all students were being pushed to prepare for college. This evidence came from the 2007 survey, where students answered questions about the degree to which teachers in the school pushed all students to plan for the future, where teachers made sure all students were planning for life after graduation, where high school classes were seen as college preparation, and students were encouraged to go to college.

Teachers also responded to questions about whether their school has expectations for most students to go to college, whether the curriculum at the school is focused on helping students get ready for college, and whether teachers in the school feel it is a part of their job to prepare students to succeed in college. Schools where more teachers endorsed these items also showed higher ACT scores than schools serving similar students where few teachers felt the school held high expectations for postsecondary education. These relationships do not just emerge because high-performing schools are those

TABLE 5

Specific classroom practices were related to ACT scores

Difference in average ACT scores between classrooms that did the activity once a month or more, compared to classrooms that did the activity less than once a month:

In English Class:	English Subtest
• Rewrote a paper or essay in response to comments	.19**
• Discussed how culture, time, or place affects an author's writing	.27**
• Explained how writers use tools like symbolism and metaphor to communicate meaning	.35***
• Improved a piece of writing as a class or with partners	.38***
• Debated the meaning of a reading	.22**
Across all classes, the students wrote papers defending their point of view of ideas five or more times (compared to less than five)[1]	.39***

In Math Class:	Math Subtest
• Discussed possible solutions to problems with other students	.29***
• Used a graphing calculator to complete an assignment	.31***

In English Class:	Reading Subtest
• Discussed how culture, time, or place affects an author's writing	.19*
• Debated the meaning of a reading	.17*

In Science Class:	Science Subtest
• Used laboratory equipment or specimens	.16**
• Wrote lab reports	.12^
• Generated their own hypothesis	.18**
• Used evidence/data to support an argument or hypothesis	.21**
• Found information from graphs and tables	.19*

Classrooms are characterized based on students' responses to questions about how often they did various instructional activities in their English, math and science classes. The differences control for students' 11th grade PLAN scores, student background characteristics, classroom and school composition, as described in Appendix D.

^p < .10   *p < .05   **p < .01   ***p < .001

[1]This difference compares students who said they were assigned five or more papers compared to students who said they were assigned less than five papers across all classes. It was calculated at the student level, rather than the classroom level.

that push students to prepare for college. As shown in Figure 28, even schools serving very disadvantaged student populations vary substantially in the degree to which they push students to prepare for college and life after high school.

To demonstrate the degree to which student effort and school climate can make a difference in students' preparation for college and the ACT, Figure 30 shows

FIGURE 29

ACT scores are highest in schools that emphasize preparation for college, comparing schools that serve similar students

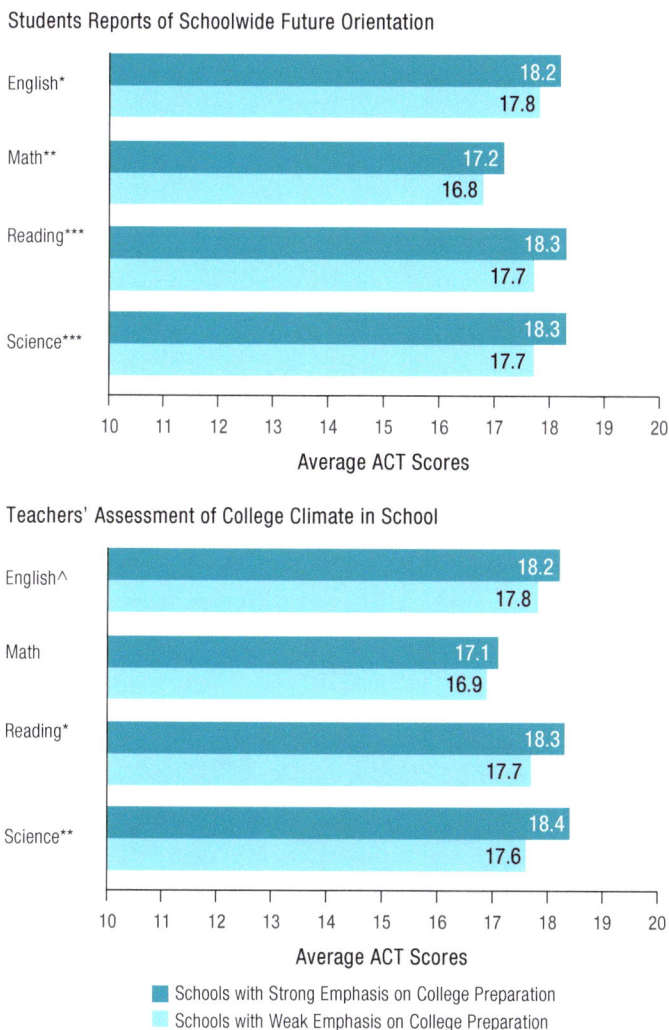

Students Reports of Schoolwide Future Orientation

English*
18.2
17.8

Math**
17.2
16.8

Reading***
18.3
17.7

Science***
18.3
17.7

Average ACT Scores

Teachers' Assessment of College Climate in School

English^
18.2
17.8

Math
17.1
16.9

Reading*
18.3
17.7

Science**
18.4
17.6

Average ACT Scores

■ Schools with Strong Emphasis on College Preparation
■ Schools with Weak Emphasis on College Preparation

Note: These differences control for students' 11th grade PLAN score, backgrounds, teacher and school characteristics, as described in Appendix D. Students' reports come from questions asking how much students agree that at their school: teachers make sure that all students are planning for life after graduation, teachers work hard to make sure that all students are learning, high school is seen as preparation for the future, all students are encouraged to go to college, teachers pay attention to all students not just the top students, and teachers work hard to make sure that students stay in school. Teachers' reports come from questions asking the extent to which they agree that: teachers expect most students in this school to go to college, teachers at this school help students plan for college outside of class time, the curriculum at this school is focused on helping students get ready for college, most of the students in this school are planning to go to college, and teachers in this school feel that it is part of their job to prepare students to suceed in college.
^p< .10 *p< .05 **p< .01 ***p< .001

average ACT scores based on the grades students received across their classes from ninth to eleventh grade and the degree to which students' and teachers' reports of school climate were strong (student reports of schoolwide future orientation and teacher reports of students' academic behaviors). Two types of students are used to illustrate the combined relationships of grades and school climate; a ninth-grader entering high school with an EXPLORE score of 14 represents a typical score for an African American student, while a ninth-grader with an EXPLORE score of 17 is on target for meeting the ACT benchmark scores by eleventh grade.[63]

Students entering ninth grade with EXPLORE scores of 17, who seem to be on-track to meet ACT benchmark scores, get average ACT composite scores close to 21 (the benchmark score for reading, and close to the benchmark score for math)—but only if they obtain B averages or better in their classes and are in schools with strong academic climates oriented towards preparing students to the future. Those without a strong GPA who attend schools with a good climate or who simply have a high GPA in a school with poor climate, come close to meeting the district goal of a composite score of 20 or above. However, even students who seemed on-track for meeting ACT benchmark scores as freshmen were unlikely to do so if they did not receive good grades in their classes and if they attended schools with climates that were not conducive to preparing students for college; their average ACT score was 18.9.

Students entering ninth grade with an EXPLORE score of 14, more typical for CPS students, were unlikely to make the district goal of a score of 20 on the ACT, even if they received high grades in their classes and attended a school with a particularly strong academic climate. However, succeeding in their courses and attending strong schools made a difference for these students—obtaining a score of 17, rather than 15, puts them in the range of access to somewhat selective colleges and makes them eligible for some scholarships.[64] In contrast, students with low GPAs who attended schools with climates that were not conducive for preparing students for college averaged ACT scores of only about 15.5. Unfortunately, for the typical student entering ninth grade with a low EXPLORE score, this latter case is the most common.

Ultimately, there are no quick fixes to bring about high ACT scores. Devoting substantial time to test practice and strategies does not improve scores. What matters is the quality of instruction and students' engagement in their classes. Furthermore, the responsibility for developing students' academic skills to do well on the ACT cannot wait until the eleventh grade. Even the best instructional practice is unlikely to produce a multipoint boost in students' scores with just six months of eleventh-grade instruction. This requires change in instructional practice throughout high school and also in the elementary and middle grades.

FIGURE 30

Students' effort in their course and school practice matter for ACT scores

ACT Scores by Students' Cumulative GPA and School Climate

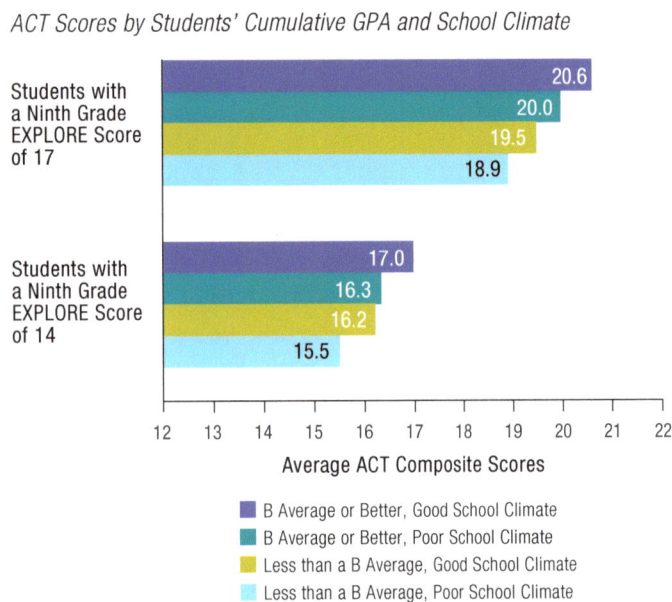

Note: "Good School Climate" is defined as being at least a half of a standard deviation above average on teachers' reports of students' behavior and above average students' reports of school-wide future orientation. "Poor School Climate" is defined as being at least a half of a standard deviation below average on teachers' reports of students' behavior and below average on students' reports of school-wide future orientation.
Among students with an EXPLORE score of 14: 25% had B averages or better, 14% had both the high GPAs *and* were in a school with a good climate.
Among students with an EXPLORE score of 17: 49% had B averages or better, 47% had both the high GPAs *and* were in a school with a good climate.

How Can We Better Address Low Performance on the ACT?

In this report, we have pointed out a number of ACT preparation problems. Yet, the responses of schools, teachers, and students are logical responses to common perceptions of the ACT. It makes sense that practicing test questions should increase scores—this should improve familiarity with test format.[65] It makes sense that the PLAN is good practice for the ACT—it has been sold to schools as a "pre-ACT." It makes sense that testing strategies can substantially improve ACT scores—we see constant advertisements from test preparation companies asserting that these strategies help. It makes sense to try to cover all of the skills in the ACT teacher guides in the months before the ACT—these are the skills being tested. However, these common perceptions do not hold up as good practice under close scrutiny. It is hard to change conventional practice when such change contradicts common wisdom, especially when the stakes are so high for students and for schools. Instead of making recommendations to educators, we outline a series of questions and considerations about preparing students for the ACT.

- **Do students understand the connection between their scores on the ACT and the work they do in their courses?**
  One of the purposes of high-stakes testing is to motivate students to work hard in school.[66] Several years ago, CCSR studied the CPS policy that enacted test score criteria for promotion from grades 3, 6, and 8. In that research, one of the most positive outcomes of the high-stakes tests was to motivate students to work hard in their classes and get support from their teachers and parents.[67] In eleventh grade, we also see that CPS students are highly motivated to do well on the ACT. Yet, teachers are channeling this motivation toward hard work on test strategies and test practice, not toward academic course work. Students and teachers see the ACT as based on test gaming, test strategies, and desire rather than academic skills or college readiness. Yet, ACT scores are much more strongly affected by students' learning in their classes than by gaming and strategies. Students are not getting the benefit of their academic

motivation, because they view the test as disconnected from what they are doing in class. Students need to get the message that the work they do in their classes, especially the really demanding work, matters for their ACT scores. ACT performance is related to grades and skill development. The emphasis on testing strategies is counterproductive—it makes students think their course work doesn't matter.

Is there a way to preserve class time for challenging academic work, while still making sure students are familiar with the ACT?

Students need some familiarity with the test before they take it so that they are ready for its structure, content, and pacing. Familiarity with the English portion of the exam seems particularly important, likely because its structure is very different from work students are used to doing in class. At the same time, it is clear that requiring teachers to spend large amounts of instructional time on practice tests is counterproductive. First, there are limits to the degree to which increasing familiarity with the testing structure can improve students' scores once they have a basic idea of the structure, content, and pacing. Second, much of the in-class test preparation does not give students a real sense of the test. Most importantly, students need to do complex academic work to prepare for the ACT. The more that class time is devoted to superficial test preparation, the less class time is available for engaging, relevant instructional tasks that will help students develop the problem-solving and complex reasoning skills tested on the ACT.

Are students getting a true sense of the test when they prepare for it?

Despite the substantial amount of time students spend preparing for the ACT, many are surprised at the length and difficulty of the exam when they take it, and they have substantial misperceptions about their probable scores. Much of the practice they receive in class has no time element, and often the practice items do not come from real practice ACT tests but from the PLAN exam or other sources. This work does not help with pacing or test familiarity. Using the PLAN as a "practice ACT" gives students a false sense of the test content, leaving them unaware of the skills they lack. Because of misperceptions about the PLAN, students do not have a realistic perception of where they are in terms of their skills or their scores, and this leads to false expectations about how they will perform on the ACT. Time spent practicing for the test should give students a real sense of the content and pacing, and should help them recognize where their skill level is and what types of academic skills they need to master to improve their score.

To what extent are teachers in earlier grades incorporating the skills students will eventually need on the ACT?

By eleventh grade, students' likelihood of substantially improving their skills for the ACT is severely constrained. The typical student gains less than one point from their score on the PLAN in the beginning of eleventh grade to their score on the ACT in the spring of eleventh grade. Yet, most of the pressure to improve students' ACT scores is placed on eleventh-grade teachers. The problem-solving, analytic, and research skills that students need on the ACT should be learned throughout high school. There also needs to be alignment between the preparation students receive in the middle grades and the skills they will need to eventually meet the ACT benchmarks. Eighth-grade students may seem prepared because they are reaching ISAT benchmarks or national norms; however, these standards represent skill levels below those needed to have a good chance of performing well on the ACT.[68] Seventh- and eighth-grade teachers need to be aware of the skills that students should possess to be ready for the current standards of rigorous high school work.

How well are courses structured to align with the skills students will need in college and for the ACT?

The ACT does not correspond with the traditional way of teaching high school subjects. It tests the deep problem-solving skills students will need in college, not the discrete facts taught in individual classes. The problems with the ACT mirror the mismatch in teaching goals and pedagogy in high school classrooms compared to college classrooms. This disconnect has been identified by researchers at ACT, Inc.; academic researchers at the Center for Educational Policy Research at the University of Oregon; and observations of researchers in the Chicago Postsecondary Transition Project.[69] Where there is mismatch between high school and college teachers' beliefs about the skills students need, ACT, Inc., has made the decision to structure the test according to the reports of college instructors, rather than those of high school teachers.[70]

If high school is to prepare students for the ACT and college, there are serious implications for the way core subjects are taught.[71] ACT, Inc., provides detailed descriptions of the skills college instructors view as important, which it uses to guide the construction of the ACT. In writing, they note that college instructors are more likely than high school teachers to demand solid knowledge of writing mechanics.[72] This is consistent with research findings that writing is one of the key content areas that students need to succeed in college.[73] In math, ACT finds that postsecondary instructors want students to have a rigorous understanding of fundamentals more than a broad knowledge of mathematical content. ACT, Inc., suggests that all high school courses should teach students to read increasingly complex texts and to develop appropriate reading strategies. Yet, they also find there is rarely much instruction on reading strategies after ninth grade.[74] Furthermore, most students are not exposed to enough nonfiction reading, but ACT incorporates nonfiction passages in many subject tests.[75] In high school, science and social science teachers tend to focus on learning facts. But postsecondary instructors are more likely to value process and inquiry skills—and these are what are tested on the ACT. Teachers will need substantial support if they are to change their pedagogies to be more consistent with the ACT and the demands of college. This will require changes across the high school curriculum, not just among eleventh-grade teachers.

Chapter 4

Why Doesn't This Accountability Test of High-Level Skills with Real-World Consequences Improve Instructional Practice?

There is a great deal of research that shows problematic effects of test-based accountability on instructional practice. High-stakes tests can cause teachers to narrow their curriculum away from non-tested topics, lose instructional time to test preparation, spend less time on instructional strategies other than test-taking, and spend less time on tasks that require students to use complex reasoning.[76] These adverse testing effects are seen most strongly in high-minority, urban schools with low average test scores, where teachers and staff are most anxious about showing improvements on the tests.[77] Yet, much of the concern with test-based accountability concerns the shallow, basic skills required for the tests.

Testing advocates have suggested that there may be beneficial effects of high-stakes tests if the tests are designed to capture appropriate high-level skills.[78] The ACT, with its emphasis on higher-order problem-solving skills, seems to be the type of test that should encourage instruction that develops deep, complex work. The real-world consequences for students make it a test that has meaning beyond the school, which should give it greater validity in the minds of teachers and students. Because the PSAE includes additional components beyond the ACT to address aspects of the state learning standards not covered by the ACT, in theory the PSAE appears well designed to encourage deep intellectual work.

However, as we have demonstrated in this study, CPS high schools' strategies around the ACT look similar to strategies associated with low-skill accountability tests, and they have comparable adverse consequences, including loss of instructional time to test preparation and less focus on complex reasoning. Hence, difficult tests, by themselves, do not seem to be sufficient for mitigating the adverse instructional effects of test-based accountability. There are a number of reasons these strong accountability incentives do not work to produce the type of instruction that would positively affect test scores and better prepare students for college, which we briefly discuss here.

A Strong Belief in Test Preparation

First, there is a pervasive belief in the benefits of test practice and testing strategies. These beliefs are fostered by test-preparation companies, some of which post advertisements on buses and billboards claiming guaranteed boosts in scores by using their methods. It is widely believed that suburban students enroll in the courses offered by these companies, and giving urban students access to those strategies may be seen as a means of equalizing opportunity. In addition, test-based accountability has a long history in Chicago, and teachers and administrators may have seen benefits from test practice and focused instruction on more basic exams given in the past.

The strong belief in the benefits of test practice, together with the intense real-world consequences for students, makes the focus on test preparation particularly insidious. If the consequences for students were not so high, some students and teachers might resist spending so much time reviewing test items and testing strategies. Since students view it as *very* important to their futures (for scholarships and college acceptance), they want to spend a lot of time preparing for it, even if they find it boring to do so. Likewise, teachers ignore their concerns about the effects of test preparation on course coverage because they want to do all they can to assure their students are prepared for the test.

"Do I think it's the best use of time in high school? No, not really, but for what we needed to accomplish, yeah."—Teacher

"So, it got to the point where we had maybe two days or one day of content for the course and then two days of ACT prep. And I do think ACT prep is important."—Teacher

The fact that the ACT is a college entrance exam has some positive effects on classroom climate; it brings teachers and students together towards a common goal, increasing motivation and strengthening teacher-student relationships. Students want to learn about college, and both teachers and students express excitement about it. Students feel very supported by their teachers around the ACT. But while there is benefit in the togetherness that accompanies the shared ACT goal, it also leads teachers and students to spend class time on such activities as motivation and test talk instead of focusing on whether students are academically ready for college success.

Misalignment between High School Curriculum and College Expectations

A second reason that the ACT does not lead to more college-oriented instruction is that its structure is not an easy one to teach to, particularly given the traditional structure of high school courses. The ACT is designed to measure college readiness more than learning in particular high school courses. While it incorporates skills taught in high school classes, it is more of a test of thinking and problem-solving skills than a test of content knowledge. It requires change in how classes are taught, rather than what is taught. It is not particularly aligned with any eleventh-grade course, although that is where most test preparation happens. Thus, eleventh-grade teachers are uncertain how to cover the material on the ACT within the structure of their courses, and they respond with instructional methods counterproductive for their course goals and the ACT.

Issues of Capacity

A third reason emphasis on the ACT does not lead directly to more college-oriented instruction is that it requires better-trained teachers. The issue of teacher capacity is particularly salient with the use of the ACT in high school accountability. Some teachers may have never received training in teaching the skills required for this type of exam—the focus of their training may have been on delivering content. A number of teachers never took the ACT themselves and may feel particularly uncomfortable with its format.

> "I honestly have no understanding of ACT. I never took it, you know."—Eleventh-grade teacher

Other teachers may have taken the ACT, but never learned the high-level problem-solving skills that it tests over the course of their own education. At about 40 percent of CPS high schools, the average teacher entered college with an ACT score of less than 19.[79] Even if they have developed complex reasoning skills in college, teachers who left high school without these skills may not view them as instructional goals that are appropriate for high school classes.

By choosing a high-level test for accountability, the assumption among lawmakers is that teachers understand the analytic skills it tests and know how to develop these skills in students. Yet, at many schools the backgrounds and training of some teachers may not be sufficient to meet these expectations, even if they have the knowledge to teach their subject area content or the material delineated in the Illinois Learning Standards. This exam requires of teachers different knowledge and skills than have traditionally been expected. In general, students do better on the ACT when they get better grades in their classes—this suggests that, on average, classes are designed in a way that develops the skills students need for the test. However, the pace at which CPS students are developing these skills is not sufficient—on average, CPS students are not making the same progress across EPAS tests as students nationally. Many teachers need support developing instructional practices that promote complex skills and more strongly engage students in their course work.

Misalignment between Eighth-Grade Benchmarks and College-Ready Skills

Finally, the inadequate preparation that students have coming out of the middle grades makes reaching college standards unrealistic for many high schools. The eighth-grade standards are not aligned with the skills students need to be on the path to being college-ready by the end of high school—they are set too low. They give the illusion that students are entering high school more prepared than they actually are, and this puts an enormous burden on high schools that are trying to prepare students for college. To get their average student to college-readiness benchmarks, high schools that serve students with average EXPLORE scores of 14 would need their students to learn at a rate that was better than 85 percent of students nationally.[80] Given these odds, it is not surprising that high schools spend so much time on test preparation strategies in hope of seeing greater progress on their students' scores.

Does All of This Mean That the ACT/PSAE Is the Wrong Choice for School Accountability?

We are not saying that the ACT is the wrong choice for school accountability—what we are saying is that the ACT/PSAE is problematic for school accountability in many of the same ways as more basic tests and that it has some additional problems of its own. Setting a high bar with a challenging accountability exam is not a panacea to the problems seen with low-skill accountability exams. However, the ACT is a valid indicator of students' preparation for college, and preparation for college is increasingly the primary goal of CPS high schools. Embedding the ACT in the state assessment ensures that all students take the college entrance exam, which brings them one step closer to applying to and enrolling in college. Research by ACT has shown that there is disconnect between what students are taught in high school and the skills college teachers say their students need. If any test were able to change instructional practice in high schools to better match the demands of college, the ACT seems like it has the potential to do so. However, it will take more to change practice than simply incorporating this high-skill test with real-world consequences into school accountability.[81]

Chapter 5

Interpretive Summary

The vast majority of CPS students want to obtain a four-year college degree. Yet, the challenge of graduating all students college-ready is a goal that has never been met in Chicago or in the country as a whole. The poor ACT performance of most CPS graduates suggests that doing so will require substantial changes in the ways that students are taught in both elementary and high school. ACT scores in Chicago's schools have been low despite high motivation among students to do well on the test and substantial school time devoted to test preparation. The typical student performs well below the score needed to have a good chance of success in college.

Eighth- and ninth-grade tests suggest that CPS students who took the ACT were ready for traditional high school work when they began high school. Most performed as well or better than the national and state averages in math and reading. However, performance at national averages on eighth- and ninth-grade tests is too low a standard if students are to meet the ACT benchmark scores by the eleventh grade. To be ready for college they need to enter ready to do rigorous high school work.[82]

Low skill levels are particularly problematic among African American and Latino students who comprise the majority of the district. Even if they show exceptional learning gains while in high school, most CPS students would be unlikely to meet the ACT benchmarks at the end of their junior year, given their skill level at the beginning of ninth grade. Getting more students to be college-ready will require support for elementary and middle schools serving mostly Latino and African American students.[83]

Problems with poor test performance in CPS become greater during students' high school years. CPS students are not making expected improvements on the EPAS system while they are in high school, and African American and Latino students show the smallest improvements. During their high school years, most students are not developing the deep analytical and reasoning skills that they will need in college. Improving ACT scores requires a close examination of the types of work that students are doing in their high school courses to prepare them for college.

Students are highly motivated to prepare for the ACT, and they are spending substantial time doing so. Their teachers are giving up weeks, even months, of instructional time to practice test-taking skills. Yet, all of this time, effort, and motivation are directed toward activities that have little or no association with improvements in test scores. Improvements from the PLAN exam in the fall of eleventh grade to the ACT in the spring are no better—and in some cases are lower—in schools that strongly emphasize preparation for the ACT, compared to similar schools with less emphasis on test preparation. Eleventh-grade course work is being dedicated to test practice and extensive content coverage. Exams are being used as instructional tools, although they are not designed for learning. These practices steal instructional time that could be used for deep, challenging course work that actually would prepare students for the ACT and for college study.

Many teachers approach their subjects with the goal of covering broad content, but that does not develop the skills that students will need in college: making meaning out of unfamiliar passages, applying reasoning skills acquired across subjects to solve problems, and paying attention to detail.[84] Eleventh-grade teachers feel substantial pressure to get students ready for the ACT, but the ACT is not a good measure of learning in any given class in just one grade. Getting students to improve their scores means preparing them to do college-level work; this requires a close look at the ways that teachers are approaching instruction and that students are learning—in their high school and

elementary classes across subjects and across grade levels. Investments in a difficult test are unlikely to advance student learning without time and attention to course content and instruction.[85] Teachers need training, support, and time to make their course work better reflect college expectations.

Work at the CCSR on postsecondary and dropout issues consistently finds that the most successful schools are those that have strategies for pushing all students to put effort into their classwork. Many students pass their classes, but D+ effort is not sufficient to develop the problem-solving skills required in college. Only students with a B average or better have at least a 50 percent chance of graduating with a four-year college degree.[86] Students' grades also are strong determinants of making it through high school; students with less than 2.0 GPAs are at risk of not graduating.[87] As we show here, test scores are strongly affected by the work students do in their classes and the grades they receive. The more that schools can get students to engage in good academic behaviors, the better their ACT scores and their students' likelihood of succeeding in college.[88]

One way of getting students to engage in their course work is to help them see that the work they do in school will prepare them for their future goals. Schools that are able to develop a college-going culture, where students see the work they are doing in their classes as preparation for the future and where all students are pushed to prepare for life after high school, show larger improvements in scores on the EPAS tests. These schools also have higher graduation rates than expected, as students are motivated to come to class and do the work they need to accumulate course credits and graduate.[89] Schools with a strong college culture are also more likely to support students in the college search, application, and enrollment process.[90] In the end, moving ACT scores up requires the same strategies as improving graduation rates and better preparing students for college—a focus on the quality of students' work in their classes, clearly tied to their preparation for the future.

References

ACT, Inc. 2004
National Data Release. August 18, 2004. www.act.org/news/releases/2004/8-18-04.html.

ACT, Inc. 2005a
Issues in College Readiness. ACT, Iowa City, IA. www.act.org/path/policy/pdf/2005-2.pdf.

ACT, Inc. 2005b
Your Guide to the ACT. ACT, Iowa City, IA. www.act.org.

ACT, Inc. 2006/2007
Preparing for the ACT (2006/2007). ACT, Iowa City, IA.

ACT, Inc. 2006a
Ready for College and Ready for Work: Same or Different? ACT, Iowa City, IA.

ACT, Inc. 2006b
PLAN Test Content and Sample Questions. ACT, Iowa City, IA.

ACT, Inc. 2006c
2006 ACT National Score Report News Release. August 16, 2006. www.act.org/news/releases/2006/ndr.html.

ACT, Inc. 2006d
Reading between the Lines: What ACT Reveals about College Readiness in Reading. www.act.org/path/policy/pdf/reading_report.pdf. (accessed on November 16, 2007).

ACT, Inc. 2007a
The ACT Technical Manual. ACT, Iowa City, IA. www.act.org/aap/pdf/ACT_Technical_Manual.pdf.

ACT, Inc. 2007b
The PLAN Technical Manual. ACT, Iowa City, IA. www.act.org/plan/pdf/PlanTechnicalManual.pdf.

ACT, Inc. 2007c
The EXPLORE Technical Manual. ACT, Iowa City, IA. www.act.org/explore/pdf/TechManual.pdf.

ACT, Inc. 2007d
Aligning Postsecondary Expectations and High School Practice: The Gap Defined, Policy Implications of the ACT National Curriculum Survey Results, 2005–2006. ACT, Iowa City, IA.

ACT, Inc. 2007e
Rigor at Risk: Reaffirming Quality in the High School Core Curriculum. ACT, Iowa City, IA. www.act.org/path/policy/pdf/rigor_report.pdf.

Allensworth, Elaine and John Q. Easton. 2007
What Matters for Staying On-Track and Graduating in Chicago Public High Schools: A Close Look at Course Grades, Failures, and Attendance in the Freshman Year. Consortium on Chicago School Research, Chicago, IL. ccsr.uchicago.edu/content/publications.php?pub_id=116.

Amrien, Audrey L. and David C. Berliner. 2002
High-Stakes Testing, Uncertainty and Student Learning. *Education Policy Analysis Archives, 10*(18). Retrieved from epaa.asu.edu/epaa/v10n18/.

Andrews, Kevin M. and Robert L. Ziomek. 1998
Score Gains on Retesting with the ACT Assessment. ACT Research Report Series 98-7. Iowa City, IA.

Briggs, Derek C. 2001
The Effect of Admissions Test Preparation: Evidence from NELS:88. *Chance, 14*(1): 10–21.

Carnoy, M., S. Loeb, and T. Smith. 2003
The Impact of Accountability Policies in Texas High Schools. In M. Carnoy, R. Elmore, and L. Siskin (eds.), *The New Accountability: High Schools and High-Stakes Testing,* pp. 147–173. New York: Routledge Falmer.

Chicago Public Schools Department of Postsecondary Education and Student Development. 2007
One-Year College Retention for the CPS Class of 2005 for All Graduates. Chicago, IL.

Cohen, P. 2007
Debate on Ending SAT Gains Ground. *New York Times,* September 19, 2007.

Conley, David T. 2007
Toward a More Comprehensive Conception of College Readiness. Eugene, OR: Educational Policy Improvement Center.

Cronin, John, Michael Dahlin, Deborah Adkins, and C. Gage Kingsbury. 2007
The Proficiency Illusion. Washington, DC: Thomas B. Fordham Institute and Northwest Education Association. www.edexcellence.net.

Darling-Hammond, Linda and Elle Rustique-Forrester. 2005
The Consequences of Student Testing for Teaching and Teacher Quality. Chapter 12 in *Uses and Misuses of Data for Educational Accountability and Improvement. The 104th Yearbook of the National Society for the Study of Education, Part 2.* Joan L. Herman and Edward H. Haertel (eds.). Blackwell: Malden, MA.

DeAngelis, Karen J., Jennifer B. Presley, and Bradford R. White. 2005
The Distribution of Teacher Quality in Illinois. Edwardsville, IL: Illinois Education Research Council.

Educational Leadership. 1993
The Challenge of Higher Standards. *Educational Leadership 50*(5).

Farzad, Roben. 2006
The Quintessential Quant: Meet the Most Wanted Man in High Finance. *Business Week.* August 21, 2006.

Geiser, Saul and Maria Veronica Santelices. 2007
Validity of High-School Grades in Predicting Student Success Beyond the Freshman Year: High-School Record vs. Standardized Tests As Indicators of Four-Year College Outcomes. Center for Studies in Higher Education, University of California, Berkeley, Research and Occasional Paper Series: CSHE.6.07.

Haertel, Edward H. and Joan L. Herman. 2005
A Historical Perspective on Validity Arguments for Accountability Testing. Chapter 1 in *Uses and Misuses of Data for Educational Accountability and Improvement. The 104th Yearbook of the National Society for the Study of Education, Part 2.* Joan L. Herman and Edward H. Haertel (eds.). Malden, MA: Blackwell.

Hamilton, K. 2005
Big Business: Educational Testing Is a Multimillion-Dollar Industry, with Revenues Only Expected to Increase with NCLB Mandated Tests. *Black Issues in Higher Education.* June 2, 2005.

Illinois State Board of Education. 2008a
Prairie State Achievement Examination Technical Manual, draft. www.isbe.net/assessment/pdfs/2006_PSAE_tech_manual.pdf (accessed on January 30, 2008).

Illinois State Board of Education. 2008b
www.isbe.net/assessment/htmls/psae_2008_schedule.htm (accessed on January 30, 2008).

Jacob, Robin Tepper, Susan Stone, and Melissa Roderick. 2004
Ending Social Promotion: The Response of Teachers and Students. Chicago, IL: Consortium on Chicago School Research.

Kaplan. 2006
ACT with CD-ROM 2006 Edition. New York: Simon & Schuster.

Maudus, George and Marguerite Clarke. 2001
The Adverse Impact of High-Stakes Testing on Minority Students: Evidence from One Hundred Years of Test Data. Chapter 5 in *Raising Standards or Raising Barriers? Inequality and High-Stakes Testing in Public Education.* Gary Orfield and Midy L. Kornhaber (eds.). New York: Century Foundation.

Murray, C. 2007
Abolish the SAT. *The American.* July/August 2007.

National Research Council. 2003
Assessment in Support of Instruction and Learning: Bridging the Gap between Large-Scale and Classroom Assessment. Workshop Report. Committee on Assessment in Support of Instruction and Learning. Board on Testing and Assessment, Committee on Science Education K–12, Mathematical Sciences Education Board. Center for Education. Division of Behavioral and Social Sciences and Education. Washington, DC: The National Academies Press.

National Research Council. 2005
How Students Learn: History, Mathematics, and Science in the Classroom. M. Suzanne Donovan and John D. Bransford (eds.). Washington, DC: The National Academies Press.

Noble, Julie. 2004
The Effects of Using ACT Composite Score and High School Average on College Admission Decisions for Racial/Ethnic Groups. In R. Zwick (ed.), *Rethinking the SAT: The Future of Standardized Testing in University Admissions,* pp. 303–319. New York: Routledge Falmer.

Noble, Julie, Mark Davenport, Jeff Schiel, and Mary Pommerich. 1999
High School Academic and Noncognitive Variables Related to the ACT Scores of Racial/Ethnic and Gender Groups. ACT Research Report Series. Iowa City, IA.

Ponisciak, Steve. 2005
Understanding the Prairie State Achievement Exam: A Descriptive Report with Analysis of Student Performance. Chicago, IL: Consortium on Chicago School Research. ccsr.uchicago.edu/content/publications.php?pub_id=9.

Presley, Jennifer B., Bradford R. White, and Yuqin Gong. 2005
Examining the Distribution and Impact of Teacher Quality in Illinois. Edwardsville, IL: Illinois Education Research Council.

Rhoten, D., M. Carnoy, M. Chabran, and R. Elmore. 2003
The Conditions and Characteristics of Assessment and
Accountability: The Case of Four States. In M. Carnoy,
R. Elmore, and L. Siskin (eds.), *The New Accountability:
High Schools and High-Stakes Testing,* pp. 13–53. New York:
Routledge Falmer.

Roderick, Melissa, Jenny Nagaoka, and Elaine Allensworth with
Vanessa Coca, Macarena Correa, and Ginger Stoker. 2006
*From High School to the Future: A First Look at Chicago Public
School Graduates' College Enrollment, College Preparation, and
Graduation from Four-Year Colleges.* Chicago, IL: Consortium
on Chicago School Research. ccsr.uchicago.edu/content/
publications.php?pub_id=7.

Roderick, Melissa, Jenny Nagaoka, Vanessa Coca, and Eliza Moeller
with Karen Rodie, Jamiliyah Gilliam, and Desmond Patton. 2008
From High School to the Future: Potholes on the Road to College.
Chicago, IL: Consortium on Chicago School Research.
ccsr.uchicago.edu/content/publications.php?pub_id=122.

Scholes, Roberta J. and Margaret N. Lain. 1997
*The Effects of Test Preparation Activities on ACT Assessment
Scores.* Paper presented at the Annual Meeting of the American
Educational Research Association, Chicago, IL. ERIC #
ED409341.

Siskin, L. 2003
When an Irresistible Force Meets an Immovable Object:
Core Lessons about High Schools and Accountability.
In M. Carnoy, R. Elmore, and L. Siskin (eds.), *The New
Accountability: High Schools and High-Stakes Testing,* pp.
175–193. New York: Routledge Falmer.

Venezky, Richard. 2000
The Origins of the Present-Day Chasm between Adult
Literacy Needs and School Literacy Instruction. *Scientific
Studies of Reading, 4*(1): 19–39.

Weber, Rebecca. 2004
Want a Job? Hand Over Your SAT Results. *Christian Science
Monitor,* May 18, 2004.

Woodruff, David. 2003
*Relationships between EPAS Scores and College Preparatory
Course Work in High School.* Retrieved from www.act.org/
research/researchers/reports/pdf/ACT_RR2003-5.pdf.

Zwick, Rebecca. 2007
College Admission Testing. National Association for College
Admission Counseling.

Appendix A:
Sample ACT Questions

Source: *Preparing for the ACT (2006/2007).*

Sample ACT Math Questions

1. Two enterprising college students decide to start a business. They will make up and deliver helium balloon bouquets for special occasions. It will cost them $39.99 to buy a machine to fill the balloons with helium. They estimate that it will cost them $2.00 to buy the balloons, helium, and ribbons needed to make each balloon bouquet. Which of the following expressions could be used to model the total cost for producing b balloon bouquets?

   A. $ 2.00b + $39.99
   B. $37.99b$
   C. $39.99b + $ 2.00
   D. $41.99b$
   E. $79.98b$

10. The sum of the real numbers x and y is 11. Their difference is 5. What is the value of xy ?

   F. 3
   G. 5
   H. 8
   J. 24
   K. 55

16. In the figure below, $\overline{AD}$ is perpendicular to $\overline{BD}$, $\overline{AC}$ is perpendicular to $\overline{BC}$, and $\overline{AD} \cong \overline{BC}$. Which of the following congruences is NOT necessarily true?

   F. $\overline{AC} \cong \overline{BD}$
   G. $\overline{AD} \cong \overline{AE}$
   H. $\overline{AE} \cong \overline{BE}$
   J. $\angle DAB \cong \angle CBA$
   K. $\angle EAB \cong \angle EBA$

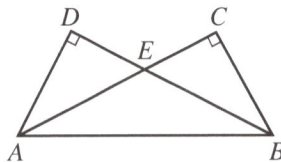

51. In teaching a lesson on the concept of thirds, Ms. Chu uses a divide-and-set-aside procedure. She starts with a certain number of colored disks, divides them into 3 equal groups, and sets 1 group aside to illustrate $\frac{1}{3}$. She repeats the procedure by taking the disks she had NOT set aside, dividing them into 3 equal groups, and setting 1 of these groups aside. If Ms. Chu wants to be able to complete the divide-and-set-aside procedure at least 4 times (without breaking any of the disks into pieces), which of the following is the minimum number of colored disks she can start with?

   A. 12
   B. 15
   C. 27
   D. 54
   E. 81

Sample ACT Science Questions

Passage I

Many bacteria contain *plasmids* (small, circular DNA molecules). Plasmids can be transferred from 1 bacterium to another. For this to occur, the plasmid *replicates* (produces a linear copy of itself). The relative position of the genes is the same on the original plasmid and on the linear copy, except that the 2 ends of the linear copy do not immediately connect.

While replication is occurring, 1 end of the linear copy leaves the donor bacterium and enters the recipient bacterium. Thus, the order in which the genes are replicated is the same as the order in which they are transferred. Unless this process is interrupted, the entire plasmid is transferred, and its 2 ends connect in the recipient bacterium.

Four students studied the way in which 6 genes (F, X, R, S, A, and G) on a specific plasmid were donated by a type of bacterium (see the figure). The students determined that the entire plasmid is transferred in 90 min and that the rate of transfer is constant. They also determined that the genes are evenly spaced around the plasmid, so 1 gene is transferred every 15 min. They disagreed, however, about the order in which the genes are replicated and thus transferred. Four models are presented.

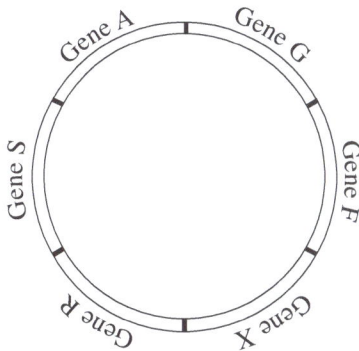

Student 1

Replication always begins between Gene F and Gene X. Gene X is replicated first and Gene F is replicated last.

Student 2

Replication always begins between Gene F and Gene X. However, the direction of replication varies. If Gene F is replicated first, Gene X is replicated last. Conversely, if Gene X is replicated first, Gene F is replicated last.

Student 3

Replication can begin between any 2 genes. Replication then proceeds around the plasmid in a clockwise direction (with respect to the figure). Thus, if Gene S is replicated first, Gene A is replicated second, and Gene R is replicated last.

Student 4

Replication can begin between any 2 genes. Likewise, replication can proceed in either direction. So the order of replication varies.

1. Based on the information presented, if the transfer of the linear copy was interrupted 50 min after transfer began, how many complete genes would have been transferred to the recipient bacterium?

   A. 2
   B. 3
   C. 4
   D. 5

2. Based on the model presented by Student 3, if all 6 genes are replicated and the first gene replicated is Gene G, the third gene replicated would be:

   F. Gene F.
   G. Gene A.
   H. Gene S.
   J. Gene X.

Sample ACT English Questions

The Music of the O'odham

[1]

For some people, traditional American Indian music is <u>associated and connected</u> with high penetrating vocals accompanied by a steady drumbeat. In tribal communities in the southwestern United States, however, one is likely to hear something similar to the polka-influenced dance music of northern Mexico. The music is called "waila." Among the O'odham tribes of Arizona, waila has been <u>popular for more than a century.</u> The music is mainly instrumental—the <u>bands generally</u> consist of guitar, bass guitar, saxophones, accordion, and drums.

[2]

Unlike some traditional tribal music, waila does not serve a religious or spiritual purpose. It is a social <u>music that performed</u> at weddings, birthday parties,

1. **A.** NO CHANGE
   B. connected by some of them
   C. linked by association
   D. associated

2. **F.** NO CHANGE
   G. popular, one might say, for
   H. really quite popular for
   J. popular for the duration of

3. Which of the following alternatives to the underlined portion would NOT be acceptable?
   A. instrumental; in general, the bands
   B. instrumental, the bands generally
   C. instrumental. The bands generally
   D. instrumental; the bands generally

4. **F.** NO CHANGE
   G. music in which it is performed
   H. music, performing
   J. music, performed

Sample ACT Reading Questions

Eleanor Roosevelt [ER] is the most controversial First Lady in United States history. Her journey to greatness, her voyage out beyond the confines of good wife and devoted mother, involved determination and
5 amazing courage. It also involved one of history's most unique partnerships. Franklin Delano Roosevelt [FDR] admired his wife, appreciated her strengths, and depended on her integrity.

However, ER and FDR had different priorities,
10 occasionally competing goals, and often disagreed. In the White House they ran two distinct and separate courts.

By 1933 [her first year as First Lady], ER was an accomplished woman who had achieved several of her
15 life's goals. With her partners, ER was a businesswoman who co-owned the Val-Kill crafts factory, a political leader who edited and copublished the *Women's Democratic News,* and an educator who co-owned and taught at a New York school for girls.

20 As First Lady, Eleanor Roosevelt did things that had never been done before. She upset race traditions, championed a New Deal for women, and on certain issues actually ran a parallel administration. On housing and the creation of model communities, for
25 example, ER made decisions and engineered policy.

At the center of a network of influential women who ran the Women's Committee of the Democratic Party led by Molly Dewson, ER worked closely with the women who had dominated the nation's social
30 reform struggles for decades. With FDR's election, the goals of the great progressive pioneers, Jane Addams, Florence Kelley, and Lillian Wald, were at last at the forefront of the country's agenda. ER's mentors since 1903, they had battled on the margins of national poli-
35 tics since the 1880s for public health, universal education, community centers, sanitation programs, and government responsibility for the welfare of the nation's poor and neglected people.

Now their views were brought directly into the White House. ER lobbied for them personally with her new administrative allies, in countless auditoriums, as a radio broadcaster, and in monthly, weekly, and, by 1936, daily columns. Called "Eleanor Everywhere," she was interested in everyone.

Every life was sacred and worthy, to be improved by education, employment, health care, and affordable housing. Her goal was simple, a life of dignity and decency for all. She was uninterested in complex theories, and demanded action for betterment. She feared violent revolution, but was not afraid of socialism—and she courted radicals.

As fascism and communism triumphed in Europe and Asia, ER and FDR were certain that there was a middle way, what ER called an American "revolution without bloodshed." Her abiding conviction, however, was that nothing good would happen to promote the people's interest unless the people themselves organized to demand government responses. A people's movement required active citizen participation, and ER's self-appointed task was to agitate and inspire community action, encourage united democratic movements for change.

Between 1933 and 1938, while the Depression raged and the New Deal unfolded, ER worked with the popular front. She called for alliances of activists to fight poverty and racism at home, and to oppose isolationism internationally.

Active with the women's peace movement, ER spoke regularly at meetings of the Women's International League for Peace and Freedom, and the Conference on the Cause and Cure of War. She departed, however, from pacifist and isolationist positions and encouraged military preparedness, collective security, and ever-widening alliances.

Between 1933 and 1938 ER published countless articles and six books. She wrote in part for herself, to clear her mind and focus her thoughts. But she also wrote to disagree with her husband. From that time to this, no other First Lady has actually rushed for her pen to jab her husband's public decisions. But ER did so routinely, including in her 1938 essay *This Troubled World,* which was a point-by-point rejection of FDR's major international decisions.

To contemplate ER's life of example and responsibility is to forestall gloom. She understood, above all, that politics is not an isolated individualist adventure. She sought alliances, created community, worked with movements for justice and peace. Against great odds, and under terrific pressure, she refused to withdraw from controversy. She brought her network of agitators and activists into the White House, and never considered a political setback a permanent defeat. She enjoyed the game, and weathered the abuse.

11. As she is revealed in the passage, ER is best described as:

   A. socially controversial but quietly cooperative.
   B. politically courageous and socially concerned.
   C. morally strong and deeply traditional.
   D. personally driven but calmly moderate.

12. The author presents ER's accomplishments as exceptional because ER:

   F. brought politically unpopular views to the forefront of the nation's politics.
   G. was the first public figure to introduce political roles for women.
   H. was a political pioneer struggling alone for social reform.
   J. replaced community action with more powerful White House networks.

13. According to the passage, ER believed that social reform should include all of the following EXCEPT:

   A. promoting community action.
   B. developing universal education.
   C. supporting affordable housing.
   D. establishing involved theories.

17. In terms of the passage as a whole, one of the main functions of the third paragraph (lines 13–19) is to suggest that:

   A. ER's successes in various professional pursuits helped prepare her to take action in the political world.
   B. ER had avoided the political spotlight in her personal pursuits.
   C. ER had competing and conflicting interests during her first year as first lady.
   D. while ER had many personal accomplishments, little could have prepared her for life as the first lady.

Appendix B:
Sample PLAN Exam Questions

Source: www.act.org/plan/pdf/sample.pdf

Sample PLAN Science Questions

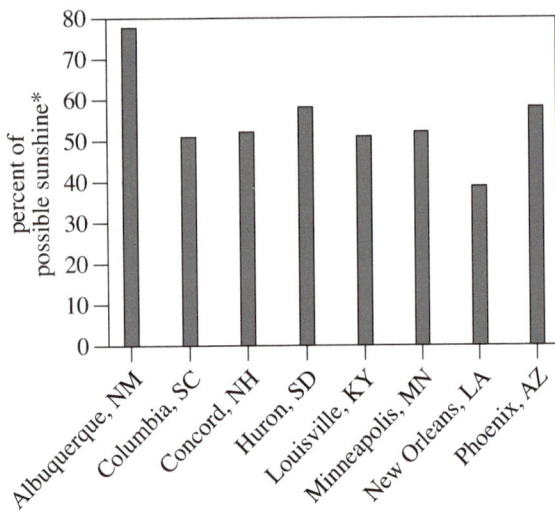

Figure 1

$$*\text{percent of possible sunshine} = \frac{\text{actual hours of direct sunlight}}{\text{possible hours of sunlight}} \times 100$$

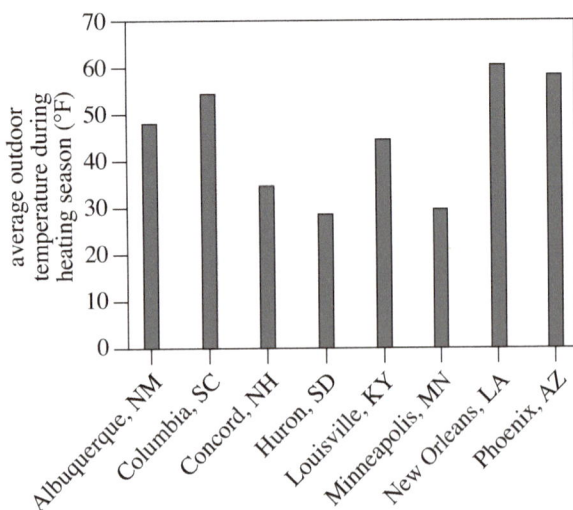

Figure 2

1. According to the information in Figure 1, which of the following cities receives the LEAST percent of possible sunshine?

   A. Albuquerque
   B. Columbia
   C. Louisville
   D. New Orleans

2. According to the information in Figure 3, the greatest heat gained through double-pane glass occurs in which of the following cities?

   F. Albuquerque
   G. Minneapolis
   H. New Orleans
   J. Phoenix

3. According to the data, the greatest net heat *loss* through a single-pane window occurred in which city?

   A. Concord
   B. Huron
   C. Minneapolis
   D. Phoenix

4. Indianapolis, Indiana, receives 51% possible sunshine and has an average temperature of 40.3°F during the heating season. On the basis of the data presented, the net heat gained by a double-pane window in Indianapolis would be approximately:

   F. -15 Btu/hr/ft^2.
   G. 7 Btu/hr/ft^2.
   H. 11 Btu/hr/ft^2.
   J. 27 Btu/hr/ft^2.

Sample PLAN Reading Questions

PROSE FICTION: This passage is adapted from Anne Tyler's novel *The Accidental Tourist* (©1985 by Anne Tyler Modarressi, et al.).

"Now, this is not your ordinary airplane," Macon told Muriel. "I wouldn't want you to get the wrong idea. This is what they call a commuter plane. It's something a businessman would take, say, to
5 hop to the nearest city for a day and make a few sales and hop back again."

The plane he was referring to—a little fifteen-seater that resembled a mosquito or a gnat—stood just outside the door of the commuters' waiting
10 room. A girl in a parka was loading it with baggage. A boy was checking something on the wings. This appeared to be an airline run by teenagers. Even the pilot was a teenager, it seemed to Macon. He entered the waiting room, carrying a clipboard. He read off a
15 list of names. "Marshall? Noble? Albright?" One by one the passengers stepped forward—just eight or ten of them. To each the pilot said, "Hey, how you doing." He let his eyes rest longest on Muriel. Either he found her the most attractive or else he was struck
20 by her outfit. She wore her highest heels, black stockings spattered with black net roses, and a flippy little fuchsia dress under a short fat coat that she referred to as her "fun fur." Her hair was caught all to one side in a great bloom of frizz, and there was a
25 silvery dust of some kind on her eyelids. Macon knew she'd overdone it, but at the same time he liked her considering this such an occasion.

The pilot propped open the door and they followed him outside, across a stretch of concrete, and
30 up two rickety steps into the plane. Macon had to bend almost double as he walked down the aisle. They threaded between two rows of single seats, each seat as spindly as a folding chair. They found spaces across from each other and settled in. Other
35 passengers struggled through, puffing and bumping into things. Last came the copilot, who had round, soft, baby cheeks and carried a can of Diet Pepsi. He slammed the door shut behind him and went up front to the controls. Not so much as a curtain hid the
40 cockpit. Macon could lean out into the aisle and see the banks of knobs and gauges, the pilot positioning his headset, the copilot taking a final swig and setting his empty can on the floor.

"Now, on a bigger plane," Macon called to
45 Muriel as the engines roared up, "you'd hardly feel the takeoff. But here you'd better brace yourself."

Muriel nodded, wide-eyed, gripping the seat ahead of her. "What's that light that's blinking in front of the pilot?" she asked.

50 "I don't know."

"What's that little needle that keeps sweeping round and round?"

"I don't know."

He felt he'd disappointed her. "I'm used to jets,
55 not these toys," he told her. She nodded again, accepting that. It occurred to Macon that he was really a very worldly and well-traveled man.

The plane started taxiing. Every pebble on the runway jolted it; every jolt sent a series of creaks
60 through the framework. They gathered speed. The crew, suddenly grave and professional, made complicated adjustments to their instruments. The wheels left the ground. "Oh!" Muriel said, and she turned to Macon with her face all lit up.

65 "We're off," he told her.

"I'm flying!"

1. Macon felt he'd disappointed Muriel because he had not:
   A. complimented her on her dress.
   B. taken her on a long trip.
   C. been able to answer her questions.
   D. chosen a more comfortable airline.

2. Which of the following sentences best describes Macon's attitude toward Muriel as it is revealed in the passage?
   F. Macon would like to impress Muriel.
   G. Macon is indifferent to Muriel.
   H. Macon resents Muriel's good looks.
   J. Macon is disappointed in Muriel.

3. When Macon compares the plane he and Muriel are on with a bigger plane (lines 39–46), he is preparing her for a:
   A. smooth takeoff.
   B. smooth flight.
   C. short flight.
   D. bumpy takeoff.

Sample PLAN Math Questions

4. In the figure below, $\overline{AB}$ is parallel to $\overline{DE}$, and $\overline{AE}$ intersects $\overline{BD}$ at C. If the measure of $\angle ABC$ is 40° and the measure of $\angle CED$ is 60°, what is the measure of $\angle BCE$?

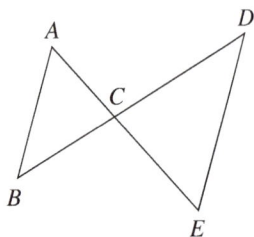

   F.   40°
   G.   60°
   H.   80°
   J.   100°
   K. 120°

5. Mark bought 3 shirts at a clothing store. Two of the shirts were priced at 2 for $15.00. If the average cost of the 3 shirts was $8.00, how much did Mark pay for the third shirt?

   A. $ 7.00
   B. $ 7.67
   C. $ 8.50
   D. $ 9.00
   E. $16.50

6. For all a and b, $6a^2b^3 - 3a^2b$ is equivalent to which of the following expressions?

   F. $3a^2b(2b^2)$
   G. $3a^2(2b^2 - 1)$
   H. $3ab(2ab^2 - 1)$
   J. $3a^2b(2b^2 - 1)$
   K. $a^2b(6b^2 - 1)$

7. In the figure below, points A, B, and C are collinear, and $\overline{AB}$ and $\overline{BC}$ are each 6 units long. If the area of $\triangle ACD$ is 24 square units, how many units long is the altitude $\overline{BD}$?

   A. 2
   B. 4
   C. 6
   D. 8
   E. 12

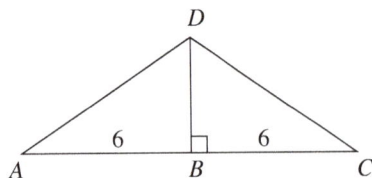

8. If $3x - 10 = 24$, then $x = ?$

   F. 31

   G. 18

   H. $11\frac{1}{3}$

   J. $4\frac{2}{3}$

   K. –2

9. Sam has some quarters, nickels, and dimes. He has 4 more quarters than dimes and 3 more dimes than nickels. If n represents the number of nickels he has, which of the following represents, in cents, the total value of all his coins?

   A. $40n + 205$
   B. $40n + 130$
   C. $40n + \ \ \ 7$
   D. $\ \ 7n + 130$
   E. $\ \ 3n + \ \ 10$

10. In $\triangle PQR$ below, $\angle PQR$ is a right angle; $\overline{PQ}$ is 3 units long; and $\overline{QR}$ is 5 units long. How many units long is $\overline{PR}$?

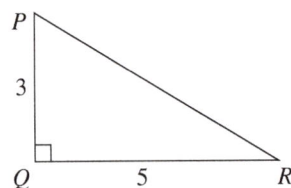

   F. 2
   G. $2\sqrt{2}$
   H. 4
   J. $\sqrt{34}$
   K. 8

11. A straight line in the coordinate plane passes through the points with (x,y) coordinates $(-1,1)$ and $(2,3)$. What are the (x,y) coordinates of the point at which the line passes through the y-axis?

   A. $(-2,0)$

   B. $(\ 0,\frac{2}{3})$

   C. $(\ 0,\frac{5}{3})$

   D. $(\ 0,2)$

   E. $(\ 0,\frac{5}{2})$

12. If the integer $5 \cdot 2^a$ is exactly divisible by just 8 positive integers, then $a = ?$

   F. 3
   G. 5
   H. 7
   J. 8
   K. 9

Appendix C:
Content of ACT Math Subject Test as Described in the ACT Teachers' Manual

Source: *Your Guide to the ACT.*

Content of the test

Items are classified according to six content areas. These categories and the approximate proportion of the test devoted to each are given in Table 4.

Table 4		
ACT Mathematics Test 60 items, 60 minutes		
Content Area	**Proportion of Test**	**Number of Items**
Pre-Algebra	.23	14
Elementary Algebra	.17	10
Intermediate Algebra	.15	9
Coordinate Geometry	.15	9
Plane Geometry	.23	14
Trigonometry	.07	4
Total	**1.00**	**60**

Scores reported:

Pre-Algebra/Elementary Algebra (24 items)
Intermediate Algebra/Coordinate Geometry (18 items)
Plane Geometry/Trigonometry (18 items)
Total test score (60 items)

1. **Pre-Algebra.** Items in this content area are based on basic operations using whole numbers, decimals, fractions, and integers; place value; square roots and approximations; the concept of exponents; scientific notation; factors; ratio, proportion, and percent; linear equations in one variable; absolute value and ordering numbers by value; elementary counting techniques and simple probability; data collection, representation, and interpretation; and understanding simple descriptive statistics.

2. **Elementary Algebra.** Items in this content area are based on properties of exponents and square roots, evaluation of algebraic expressions through substitution, using variables to express functional relationships, understanding algebraic operations, and solving quadratic equations by factoring.

3. **Intermediate Algebra.** Items in this content area are based on an understanding of the quadratic formula, rational and radical expressions, absolute value equations and inequalities, sequences and patterns, systems of equations, quadratic inequalities, functions, modeling, matrices, roots of polynomials, and complex numbers.

4. **Coordinate Geometry.** Items in this content area are based on graphing and the relations between equations and graphs, including points, lines, polynomials, circles, and other curves; graphing inequalities; slope; parallel and perpendicular lines; distance; midpoints; and conics.

5. **Plane Geometry.** Items in this content area are based on the properties and relations of plane figures, including angles and relations among perpendicular and parallel lines; properties of circles, triangles, rectangles, parallelograms, and trapezoids; transformations; the concept of proof and proof techniques; volume; and applications of geometry to three dimensions.

6. **Trigonometry.** Items in this content area are based on understanding trigonometric relations in right triangles; values and properties of trigonometric functions; graphing trigonometric functions; modeling using trigonometric functions; use of trigonometric identities; and solving trigonometric equations.

Appendix D:
Statistical Models

Models for the Analysis of Test Score Gains from the Eleventh-Grade PLAN to the ACT

The analyses that examined test score gains from the ninth-grade EXPLORE to the tenth-grade PLAN, from the tenth-grade PLAN to the eleventh-grade PLAN, and from the eleventh-grade PLAN to the ACT in spring of eleventh grade used three-level hierarchical linear models, nesting students within classrooms within schools. These models were used to analyze all subject-specific gains in test scores (Figure 20 through Figure 29 and the final five bars in Figure 14, which incorporate school effects). Analysis of composite scores used two-level models that did not include classroom-level or teacher-specific control variables. The same base models were run repeatedly with different survey indicators of test preparation included as predictors.

At Level 1, we controlled for student GPA in the relevant subject during the time period between tests (in increments of 0.5 points) and pretest score (either grade 9 EXPLORE, grade 10 PLAN, or grade 11 PLAN), and—where possible (due to limitations on the number of variables in HLM)—student race, gender, special education status, latent ITBS score measured from tests taken in grades 3 through 8, courses taken, and course absences. GPA and PLAN were entered as a series of dummy variables with interactions. At Level 2, we included teacher and classroom compositional variables, including information about the degrees a teacher received, teachers' majors, universities where they received their degrees, and student peer achievement. For the analysis of racial gaps we included variables representing students' academic track (Honors, AP, IB) and their eleventh-grade course (e.g., Algebra II, Geometry). At the school level, we initially tried a number of compositional variables, but those that remained the best predictors of ACT gains were indicators for high percentages of low-income students and magnet schools.

Level 1 Model

$$ACT_{ijk} = \pi_0 + \pi_1{}^*(\text{Latent Eighth-Grade Achievement}) + \pi_2{}^*(\text{No Latent})$$
$$+ \pi_3 \ldots \pi_7{}^*(\text{Course Indicator Dummy Variables Specific to Subject})$$
$$+ \pi_8{}^*(\text{Special Ed}) + \pi_9{}^*(\text{Black}) + \pi_{10}{}^*(\text{Native American}) + \pi_{11}{}^*(\text{Latino}) + \pi_{12}{}^*(\text{Female})$$
$$+ \pi_{13} \ldots \pi_{113}{}^*(\text{Series of Indicators of Eleventh-Grade PLAN Score x GPA Interactions})$$
$$+ \pi_{114} \ldots \pi_{129}{}^*(\text{Series of Indicators Indicating Number of Days Absent from Course}) + e$$

Level 2 Model for Intercept

$\pi_{0jk} = \beta_{00} + \beta_{01} \ldots \beta_{09}{}^*$(Series of Dummy Variables Indicating the Percentage of Students in the Class Entering High School at/above National Norms)

$+ \beta_{010}{}^*$(Doctorate) $+ \beta_{011}{}^*$(Master's)

$+ \beta_{012} \ldots \beta_{051}{}^*$(Series of Dummy Variables Indicating University Attended by Teacher)

$+ \beta_{052}{}^*$(Average Student Poverty Level in Class)

$+ \beta_{053} \ldots \beta_{072}{}^*$(Series of Dummy Variables Indicating Subject Area and Type of Degree Teacher Received) $+ r_0$

Level 3 Model for Intercept

$\beta_{00} = \gamma_{000} + \gamma_{001}{}^*$(% Low Income) $+ \gamma_{002}{}^*$(Magnet School) $+ \upsilon_{00}$

Equations for control variables were fixed at Levels 2 and 3.

Non-Nested Models for Race Analyses

OLS regression equations were used to discern differences in ACT scores by race and ethnicity without accounting for school effects. Summaries of these models are presented in Table 6. The coefficients from these models were used to graph Figure 7 and for the first three bars in Figure 9 (those bars that do not include school effects).

TABLE 6

Coefficients from non-nested models of race effects for Figure 7

	Model with just GPA as a Predictor of ACT Composite	Model with GPA and Prior Test Scores
Intercept	10.22***	15.91***
White	2.49***	0.53***
Latina/o	0.36***	0.00
Asian	2.27***	0.68***
Male	0.67***	0.27***
GPA	2.38***	0.46***
GPA over 3.5	0.83***	0.36***
Asian x GPA over 3.5	0.81*	0.09
White x GPA over 3.5	1.75***	0.64***
Latino/a x GPA over 3.5	0.29	0.17
Eighth-Grade Score		1.23***
PLAN score		0.71***

^p < .10   *p < .05   **p < .01   ***p < .001

TABLE 7

Coefficients from non-nested models of race effects for first three bars of Figure 14

	English			Math		
	Model 1	Model 2	Model 3	Model 1	Model 2	Model 3
Intercept	16.33***	16.55***	15.63***	15.70***	15.88***	15.32***
White	3.49***	2.98***	1.45***	3.92***	3.49***	1.45***
Latina/o	0.34***	0.53***	0.55***	0.98***	1.17***	0.50***
Asian	3.66***	3.31***	2.37***	5.06***	4.76***	1.63***
Male	-0.90***	-0.92***	-0.51***	0.16*	0.15*	0.11*
Poverty		-0.27***	-0.23***		-0.21***	-0.09*
Social Status		0.63***	0.11*		0.57***	0.23***
Eighth-Grade Score			4.45***			3.15***

	Reading			Science		
	Model 1	Model 2	Model 3	Model 1	Model 2	Model 3
Intercept	16.08***	16.29***	16.24***	16.85***	16.99***	16.59***
White	3.51***	3.03***	1.33***	2.98***	2.65***	1.17***
Latina/o	0.33***	0.54***	0.58***	0.53***	0.74***	0.25***
Asian	3.59***	3.26***	1.67***	3.71***	3.48***	1.21***
Male	-0.90***	-0.92***	-0.31***	0.04	0.03	0.00
Poverty		-0.24***	-0.14***		-0.14**	-0.06
Social Status		0.64***	0.17***		0.52***	0.27***
Eighth-Grade Score			4.44***			2.29***

^p < .10 *p < .05 **p < .01 ***p < .001

Appendix E:
Survey Measures Used in Analyses

Measures of Students' Behaviors

Teachers' reports of students' behavior in their class assesses whether students perform the expected tasks of class participation: coming to class on time, attending class regularly, turning in homework, and actively participating.

	High School
Individual Separation:	2.87
Individual Level Reliability:	0.89
School Level Reliability:	0.87

2007 Item Code	Item Text	Item Difficulty	Item Fit
Stu29q04	How many students in your TARGET CLASS, come to class on time? None, Some, About Half, Most, Nearly All	-0.63	1.44
Stu29q05	How many students in your TARGET CLASS, attend class regularly? None, Some, About Half, Most, Nearly All	-1.32	1.01
Stu29q06	How many students in your TARGET CLASS, come to class prepared with the appropriate supplies and books? None, Some, About Half, Most, Nearly All	0.46	0.89
Stu29q07	How many students in your TARGET CLASS, regularly pay attention in class? None, Some, About Half, Most, Nearly All	-0.22	0.73
Stu29q08	How many students in your TARGET CLASS, actively participate in class activities? None, Some, About Half, Most, Nearly All	0.08	1.05
Stu29q09	How many students in your TARGET CLASS, always turn in their homework? None, Some, About Half, Most, Nearly All	1.64	1.16

Students' reports of peers' behavior in their class asks if students' classmates treat each other with respect, work together well, help each other learn, and if other students disrupt class, like to put others down, and don't care about each other.

	Elementary	High School
Individual Separation:	1.27	1.14
Individual Level Reliability:	0.62	0.56
School Level Reliability:	0.95	0.99

2007 Item Code	Item Text	Item Difficulty	Item Fit
stu03q01	How much do you agree with the following statements about students in your school? Most students in my school don't really care about each other. Strongly Disagree, Disagree, Agree, Strongly Agree	-0.11	0.44
stu03q02	How much do you agree with the following statements about students in your school? Most students in my school like to put others down. Strongly Disagree, Disagree, Agree, Strongly Agree	0.29	0.47
stu03q03	How much do you agree with the following statements about students in your school? Most students in my school help each other learn. Strongly Disagree, Disagree, Agree, Strongly Agree	-0.27	0.64
stu03q04	How much do you agree with the following statements about students in your school? Most students in my school don't get along together very well. Strongly Disagree, Disagree, Agree, Strongly Agree	-0.15	0.48
stu03q05	How much do you agree with the following statements about students in your school? Most students in my school just look out for themselves. Strongly Disagree, Disagree, Agree, Strongly Agree	0.1	0.58
stu03q06	How much do you agree with the following statements about students in your school? Most students in my school treat each other with respect. Strongly Disagree, Disagree, Agree, Strongly Agree	0.02	0.58

Measures of College-Going Culture

Teachers' reports of expectations in the school for students' postsecondary education asks teachers whether their school has an environment that is supportive of students enrolling in college.

	High School
Individual Separation:	1.97
Individual Level Reliability:	0.79
School Level Reliability:	0.94

2007 Item Code	Item Text	Item Difficulty	Item Fit
pln21q01	**Please mark the extent to which you disagree or agree with the following:** Teachers expect most students in this school to go to college. Strongly Disagree, Disagree, Agree, Strongly Agree	0.4	0.93
pln21q02	**Please mark the extent to which you disagree or agree with the following:** Teachers at this school help students plan for college outside of class time. Strongly Disagree, Disagree, Agree, Strongly Agree	0.29	1.1
pln21q03	**Please mark the extent to which you disagree or agree with the following:** The curriculum at this school is focused on helping students get ready for college. Strongly Disagree, Disagree, Agree, Strongly Agree	-0.32	0.85
pln21q05	**Please mark the extent to which you disagree or agree with the following:** Most of the students in this school are planning to go to college. Strongly Disagree, Disagree, Agree, Strongly Agree	0.83	1.01
pln21q06	**Please mark the extent to which you disagree or agree with the following:** Teachers in this school feel that it is a part of their job to prepare students to succeed in college. Strongly Disagree, Disagree, Agree, Strongly Agree	-1.21	0.85

Students' reports of schoolwide future orientation measures students' views of school norms of academic expectations. Students report on the degree to which all students are expected to work hard, to stay in school, to plan for their futures, and to have high personal aspirations for their lives after graduation.

	High School
Individual Separation:	1.78
Individual Level Reliability:	0.76
School Level Reliability:	0.94

2007 Item Code	Item Text	Item Difficulty	Item Fit
slp37q01	How much do you agree with the following? At my high school, teachers make sure that all students are planning for life after graduation. Strongly Disagree, Disagree, Agree, Strongly Agree	0.5	0.9
slp37q02	How much do you agree with the following? At my high school, teachers work hard to make sure that all students are learning. Strongly Disagree, Disagree, Agree, Strongly Agree	0.13	0.63
slp37q03	How much do you agree with the following? At my high school, high school is seen as preparation for the future. Strongly Disagree, Disagree, Agree, Strongly Agree	-1.23	0.99
slp37q04	How much do you agree with the following? At my high school, all students are encouraged to go to college. Strongly Disagree, Disagree, Agree, Strongly Agree	-0.6	1.02
slp37q05	How much do you agree with the following? At my high school, teachers pay attention to all students, not just the top students. Strongly Disagree, Disagree, Agree, Strongly Agree	0.59	0.87
slp37q06	How much do you agree with the following? At my high school, teachers work hard to make sure that students stay in school. Strongly Disagree, Disagree, Agree, Strongly Agree	0.6	0.85

Endnotes

Introduction

1 Colleges and universities routinely state that admissions tests are only one factor of many considered for acceptance (Kaplan, 2006).

2 Weber (2004); Farzad (2006).

3 Hamilton (2005).

4 Murray (2007).

5 ACT scores have increased slightly over the last five years, but remain low. At the first administration, in 2001, the mean composite score was 16.1. Last year, the average composite score was 17.2.

6 See Haertel and Herman (2005) for a summary of the history and arguments about high-stakes testing. Also see Educational Leadership (1993) for a discussion of testing standards at the start of the current movement and a recent report that criticizes standards currently being used for state and federal accountability by Cronin, Dahlin, Adkins, and Kingsbury (2007).

7 The class of 2005 did not receive the writing portion of the ACT. Students now take the ACT Writing test in addition to the mentioned subjects.

8 ISBE also gave a social studies test as part of the PSAE up to 2004.

9 Illinois State Board of Education (2008a).

10 The exact formula for PSAE scores is available at www.isbe.net/high_school/psae_myths.ppt (accessed on January 30, 2008).

11 Illinois State Board of Education. (2008b).

12 Roderick, Nagaoka, and Allensworth (2006).

13 For example, the University of Illinois at Urbana-Champaign admits very few students with ACT scores below 23 (www.oar.uiuc.edu/future/apply/requirements_freshman.html), while University of Illinois at Chicago admits few students with ACT scores under 21 (www.uic.edu). In an internet listing of guaranteed scholarships (www.guaranteed-scholarships.com), the vast majority require an ACT score of at least 24; only a few colleges listed scholarships for students with scores below 20.

14 National and state ACT scores are reported for the Class of 2006. National statistics were accessed on April 23, 2008, at www.act.org/news/data/06/pdf/one.pdf. State statistics came from www.act.org/news/data/06/states.html, accessed on April 23, 2008.

15 ACT, Inc. (2006c).

Chapter 1

16 At the time these students took the ISAT, the reading cutoff for meeting standards was 151.5, while the math cutoff was 161.5; this was above the state average (160). The math standard has since been lowered to 146. Only about five percent of students who were at the new math standard attained a score of 20 or better on the ACT (Easton, forthcoming).

17 A work forthcoming from CCSR by John Q. Easton, "The Path to 20," provides further details on the relationships between students' elementary grade test scores and their ACT scores.

18 ACT, Inc. (2007b); ACT, Inc. (2007c).

19 Their eighth-grade ISAT scores were similar to the performance of students statewide in eighth grade: Statewide, eighth-grade reading performance was 1 percent at academic warning (compared to 1 percent in CPS), 31 percent below expectations (compared to 35 percent in CPS), 58 percent meeting expectations (compared to 58 percent in CPS), and 10 percent exceeding standards (compared to 6 percent in CPS). Statewide eighth-grade math performance was 7 percent at academic warning (compared to 8 percent in CPS), 40 percent below expectations (compared to 52 percent in CPS), 37 percent meeting expectations (compared to 32 percent in CPS), and 15 percent exceeding standards (compared to 7 percent in CPS). State numbers were taken from the website of the Illinois State Board of Education (www.isbe.net).

20 The percentage of students meeting the ISAT standards in math was similar to those meeting the EXPLORE benchmark, suggesting that in 2002 the math standards were on par with expectations on the ACT system. However, the math standard in Illinois has since been lowered.

21 ACT, Inc. (2007b); ACT, Inc. (2007c).

22 In our interviews, for example, some teachers wondered why their students' scores were so low and hypothesized that there were racial biases in the tests so that the scores did not truly capture students' skills.

23 Roderick et al (2006); Geiser and Santelices (2007); Noble (2004); Zwick (2007).

24 ACT, Inc. 2007. www.act.org/news/data/05/pdf/t1-2.pdf (accessed on September 7, 2007).

25 ACT, Inc. (2005a).

26 Chicago Public Schools Department of Postsecondary Education and Student Development (2007).

27 While the vast majority of students of all ability levels felt that it was important to do well on the ACT, the students who disagreed that the ACT was important were more likely to be high-achieving students than low-achieving students. Students entering high school at norms were twice as likely as students entering two years below norms to strongly disagree that the ACT was important, perhaps because good ACT scores were less crucial for them to gain acceptance to college, given that they likely had higher grades.

28 Work Keys scores are reported as levels: lower than 3, 3, 4, 5, 6, and 7. In 2007, more students scored a 4 than in 2006, and fewer students scored above a 4, especially in reading.

29 A graphical representation of the relationship between ACT scores and Work Keys scores in CPS in 2004 can be found in Ponisciak (2005). Scores in 2007 also show a very strong correspondence, so that almost all of the scores of 3 or lower on Work Keys occur among students with ACT scores lower than 18.

30 ACT, Inc. (2006a).

31 Briggs (2001).

32 Scholes and Lain (1997).

33 One source, for example, suggests reading the exam questions before reading the passages that accompany the questions, while another source recommends reading the passages thoroughly before reading the questions.

34 In fact, college entrance exams seem to over-predict the college performance of minority students. Most pertinent to this subject is a study on the ACT by Noble (2004), who finds that the ACT does not under-predict college performance among minority students, and that the ACT is an even better predictor of college performance among African American students than among white students. Within this work, Noble cites other research that also shows that the ACT does not under-predict minority students' college performance. Further discussion of this issue is available in Zwick (2007).

35 ACT, Inc. (2007d).

36 Noble, Davenport, Schiel, and Pommerich (1999).

37 They conclude that there are no significant race effects after they control for grades, high school program, self-evaluation of skills, and high school. There are two problems with these conclusions. First, they control for variables that are likely a result of students' actual performance—self-appraisal of their skills that occurs after taking the ACT. If African American and Latino students struggled more on the test than white students did, this would likely affect their self-appraisals. Second, the race coefficients remain large even though they are statistically nonsignificant; they become statistically nonsignificant because of multicollinearity with other predictors in the model.

38 In a previous CCSR report (Allensworth and Easton, 2007), we found that freshman grades were much more strongly associated with attendance and effort than with prior academic ability.

39 Economic status is measured with an indicator of whether the student received free or reduced lunch and with variables that describe the economic conditions in students' residential block groups—the percentage of families in poverty, the male unemployment rate, the average income, and the average education level.

Chapter 2

40 Kaplan (2006), p. 27.

41 Description provided on their website, www.act.org/plan/index.html.

42 ACT, Inc. (2006b).

43 ACT, Inc. (2005b).

44 ACT, Inc. (2007b).

45 The benefits of retesting are small and diminish the more times students take the test. Overall, only half of students who take the ACT a second time improve their scores—the other half receive the same or lower score. The average gain is 0.7 points on the first retake, 0.6 on the second, and 0.5 on the third (Andrews and Ziomek, 1998).

46 Retrieved on April 3, 2008, from www.actstudent.org/regist/retake.html.

47 ACT, Inc. (2005b).

48 ACT, Inc. (2007a).

49 ACT, Inc. (2007a).

50 ACT, Inc. (2007b).

51 ACT, Inc. (2007b).

52 Conley (2007).

53 ACT, Inc. (2005b).

54 ACT, Inc. (2007d).

55 This is consistent with the Illinois Learning Standards for late high school literature (www.isbe.net/ils/ela/standards.htm).

56 The ACT curriculum study found that high school science teachers rate science content as more important than science process/inquiry skills, while postsecondary science teachers rate science process skills as more important than science content (ACT, Inc., 2007d).

57 National Research Council (2005). Carnoy, Loeb, and Smith (2003).

58 Not only were the differences between those who attended occasionally and never attended insignificant, but they were also very small (under 0.1) and negative in reading.

59 Schools ranged from zero to half of eleventh-graders attending an ACT preparatory class outside of school hours.

60 There were negative relationships between the percentage of students attending an ACT preparation class often and school average ACT scores in all subjects, controlling for student and school characteristics as described in Appendix D. Only with the average math scores did the relationship reach a level of statistical significance (p = .002). Visual examination of school residual math scores with the percentage of students attending a preparation class showed a consistently negative relationship at all levels of preparation class attendance, and all schools with a quarter or more of eleventh-graders attending a preparation class outside of school showed math residuals that were below the system average.

61 Andrews and Ziomek (1998). These figures are based on actual ACT tests and incorporate effects of preparation activities that students may have done between test administrations.

62 We did these comparisons at both the student and classroom level. At the student level, many of the items showed negative relationships with reading scores, but in an inconsistent way. For example, scores would be lower among students who reported "some" than those who reported "none," but not different for those who reported "a great deal" compared to "none."

Chapter 3

63 About one-quarter (24 percent) of students with an EXPLORE score of 14 had a GPA of B (3.0) or better as of the spring semester of their junior year; about half (49 percent) of students with an EXPLORE score of 17 had a B average or better. About 14 percent of students with an EXPLORE score of 14 had a B average and were in schools with good climate; 47 percent of students with an EXPLORE score of 17 had B averages or better and were in schools with a good climate.

64 Patterns of access to different types of colleges by students' ACT scores and GPAs are described in Roderick, Nagaoka, and Allensworth (2006).

65 There are common misperceptions that ACT and SAT scores are strongly influenced by test preparation; the College Board and the dean of admission at Harvard University agree that urban legends about test preparation need to be addressed (Cohen, 2007).

66 See Amrien and Berliner (2002) for a summary of issues around high-stakes testing.

67 Jacob, Stone, and Roderick (2004).

68 Further details will be provided in the forthcoming CCSR report "The Path to 20" by John Q. Easton.

69 ACT, Inc., found that high school teachers emphasize broad content knowledge, while college instructors say students need a thorough understanding of basic concepts (ACT, Inc., 2007d). Conley (2007) at the University of Oregon found that college classes tend to emphasize key thinking skills such as being able to make inferences, interpret results, analyze conflicting explanations, support arguments with evidence, and solve complex problems, but these skills are rarely developed in high school. Likewise, interviews of college professors of our interviewees have noted that students need problem-solving skills more than content.

70 ACT, Inc. (2007d).

71 A number of recent initiatives in specific CPS high schools are purposely aligned with the skills students will need in college and on the ACT. The IDS programs, for example, are structured specifically to prepare students for the ACT.

72 ACT, Inc. (2007d).

73 Conley (2007).

74 ACT, Inc. (2006d).

75 Venezky (2000).

Chapter 4

76 Darling-Hammond and Rustique-Forrester (2005).

77 Rhoten, Carnoy, Chabran, and Elmore (2003): Maudus and Clarke (2001).

78 See Educational Leadership (1993); Cronin, Dahlin, Adkins, and Kingsbury (2007); Haertel and Herman (2005).

79 This is an estimate based on the TQI indicator developed by researchers at the Illinois Education Research Council. This indicator measures human capital characteristics of teachers and incorporates the ACT as one of its major components. IERC researchers showed that 26 of 69 CPS high schools had average TQI of less than -1, with a few CPS high schools averaging a TQI of less than -2 (DeAngelis, Presley, and White, 2005). A TQI of -1 corresponds to an ACT score of about 19.4, while a TQI of -2 corresponds to an ACT score of about 18.1 (Presley, White, and Gong, 2005). Researchers at the Illinois Education Research Council found that high school teachers' own educational backgrounds (i.e., their own ACT scores) were strongly related to their students' test scores (Presley, White, and Gong, 2005).

80 This probability is extrapolated from figures available from ACT and is likely a low estimate—it is actually probably even harder. According to Woodruff (2003), the typical eleventh-grade ACT score for a student with an eighth-grade EXPLORE score of 14 is between 18.0 and 18.7, depending on their high school course work, with a standard deviation of 2.3 or 2.47. Thus, to score a 21 on the ACT (which is around the benchmarks), students with a 14 on the eighth-grade EXPLORE would need to show improvements that were about one standard deviation above the mean, approximately in the top 15 percent. Students with an EXPLORE score of 14 in ninth grade, instead of the eighth grade, would likely have an even smaller likelihood of reaching a score of 21 by the end of their junior year. Students with less than a 14 would have a yet smaller likelihood of reaching a score of 21.

81 A National Research Council work group (2003) found that it was rare for large-scale assessments to be aligned well with classroom assessments and instruction, but that the programs that seemed most promising included these specific elements: high responsibility among teachers to change their thinking and practice; sustained high levels of professional development; detailed descriptions of expectations for students; substantial feedback to teachers and students; and adherence to high professional standards.

Chapter 5

82 ACT also argues that too few students nationwide meet EXPLORE benchmarks (ACT, Inc., 2007e, p. 12).

83 Research in Texas also shows that when students are two or three years behind in elementary school, this unpreparedness becomes five or six years in high school. Siskin (2003).

84 Conley (2007) has identified what he calls "habits of mind" to refer to the intellectual behaviors needed for college, which include intellectual openness, inquisitiveness, analysis, reasoning/argumentation/proof, interpretation, precision and accuracy, and problem solving.

85 See Siskin (2003).

86 Roderick, Nagaoka, and Allensworth (2006).

87 Allensworth and Easton (2007).

88 Allensworth and Easton (2007).

89 Allensworth and Easton (2007).

90 Roderick, Nagaoka, Coca, and Moeller (2008).

About the Authors

Elaine Allensworth

Elaine Allensworth is the Co-Director for Statistical Analysis at the Consortium on Chicago School Research at the University of Chicago. She holds a PhD in sociology and an MA in sociology and urban studies from Michigan State University. Allensworth is an expert in statistical methodology, but she believes that knowledge develops best by combining qualitative and quantitative methods. Her research examines the structural factors that affect high school students' educational attainment. She has written a number of reports on graduation rates in the Chicago Public Schools, including *What Matters for Staying On-Track and Graduating in Chicago Public Schools* (2007), *The On-Track Indicator as a Predictor of High School Graduation* (2005), *Graduation and Dropout Trends in Chicago: A Look at Cohorts of Students from 1991 to 2004* (2005), and *Ending Social Promotion: Dropout Rates in Chicago after Implementation of the Eighth-Grade Promotion Gate* (2004). She recently began a three-year mixed-methods study of the transition to high school that looks at students' perceptions of the challenges of high school, the school practices that can foster successful freshman-year performance and the practices that can hinder students. She also is leading several studies on the effects of rigorous curricula on students' experiences in their classes, grades, test scores, high school graduation and college attendance. Allensworth is a member of the CCSR Chicago Postsecondary Transition Project, which is interviewing students as they move from their junior year in high school through their first two years of college and work. Her concern with the low ACT scores of students being interviewed for this project led her to do this work on students' performance on the ACT. She once was a high school Spanish and science teacher.

Macarena Correa

Macarena Correa is a Research Analyst at CCSR. Correa received her BA in psychology from Harvard College and her EdM from the Harvard Graduate School of Education (HGSE) where her focus was administration, planning, and social policy. She also participated in the undergraduate teacher education program at HGSE. Her interests lie in improving teaching conditions, professional development and the achievement gap.

Steve Ponisciak

Steve Ponisciak is an Associate Researcher at the Wisconsin Center for Education Research (WCER). He works in the Value Added Research Center at WCER and in the Department of Applied Research at Chicago Public Schools. At CCSR, Ponisciak was a senior research analyst. He analyzed the PSAE, ACT, EXPLORE, and PLAN tests; studied teacher mobility in CPS; and worked on value-added models for school performance. Ponisciak earned a BS in mathematics from the University of Notre Dame and earned his PhD from the Institute of Statistics and Decision Sciences at Duke University, where his dissertation was focused on Bayesian analysis of teacher effectiveness.

This report reflects the interpretation of the authors. Although the CCSR's Steering Committee provided technical advice and reviewed earlier versions, no formal endorsement by these individuals, organizations, or the full Consortium should be assumed.

This report was produced by CCSR's publications and communications staff.

Editing and project management by Publications & Creative Services
Graphic design by Jeff Hall Design
Photos by David Schalliol

5-08/1.5M/OTH08076

Consortium on Chicago School Research

Directors

John Q. Easton
Executive Director
Consortium on Chicago
School Research

Elaine Allensworth
Consortium on Chicago
School Research

Melissa Roderick
University of Chicago

Penny Bender Sebring
Consortium on Chicago
School Research

Steering Committee

Josie Yanguas, *Co-Chair*
Illinois Resource Center

Steve Zemelman, *Co-Chair*
Illinois Network of Charter
Schools

Institutional Members

Clarice Berry
Chicago Principals and
Administrators Association

Barbara Eason-Watkins
Steve Washington
Ginger Reynolds
Chicago Public Schools

Marilyn Stewart
Chicago Teachers Union

Individual Members

Veronica Anderson
Catalyst Chicago

Gina Burkhardt
Learning Point Associates

Carolyn Epps
Chicago Public Schools

Timothy Knowles
Center for Urban
School Improvement

Janet Knupp
Chicago Public
Education Fund

Mark Larson
National Louis University

Carol D. Lee
Northwestern University

George Lowery
Roosevelt University

Peter Martinez
University of Illinois
at Chicago

Ruanda Garth McCullough
Loyola University

Gregory Michie
Illinois State University

Stephen Raudenbush
University of Chicago

Brian Spittle
DePaul University

Matthew Stagner
Chapin Hall Center
for Children

Kim Zalent
Business and Professional
People for the Public Interest

Martha Zurita
Latino Youth Alternative
High School

Our Mission

The Consortium on Chicago School Research (CCSR) at the University of Chicago conducts research of high technical quality that can inform and assess policy and practice in the Chicago Public Schools. We seek to expand communication among researchers, policy makers, and practitioners as we support the search for solutions to the problems of school reform. CCSR encourages the use of research in policy action and improvement of practice, but does not argue for particular policies or programs. Rather, we help to build capacity for school reform by identifying what matters for student success and school improvement, creating critical indicators to chart progress, and conducting theory-driven evaluation to identify how programs and policies are working.

www.ingramcontent.com/pod-product-compliance
Lightning Source LLC
Chambersburg PA
CBHW042015080426
42735CB00002B/57